HEALING STRESS, ANXIETY AND DEPRESSION

Liber your mind from negative thoughts, overcome your fears, take control of your life and find the joy of living once and for all without the use of drugs

By

Alicia J. Parker

otherwise, by any usage or abuse of any policies, processes, or directions contained within is the solitary and utter responsibility of the recipient reader. Under no circumstances will any legal responsibility or blame be held against the publisher for any reparation, damages, or monetary loss due to the information herein, either directly or indirectly.

Respective authors own all copyrights not held by the publisher.

The information herein is offered for informational purposes solely, and is universal as so. The presentation of the information is without contract or any type of guarantee assurance.

The trademarks that are used are without any consent, and the publication of the trademark is without permission or backing by the trademark owner. All trademarks and brands within this book are for clarifying purposes only and are the owned by the owners themselves, not affiliated with this document.

Table of Contents

Chapter 1

UNDERSTANDING ANXIETY DISORDER

In medical terminology, anxiety disorder generally relates to a state of nervousness or discomfort. Anxiety disorder is one of the most prevalent illnesses in mental health. It is described as a critical mental disorder that can eventually contribute to chronic anxiety. It generally occurs because of job stress, a very limited job schedule that tends to interrupt the mood or conduct of an individual. However, if adequate anxiety treatment is not well pursued in moment, it can even damage a person's mental state.

An individual suffering from anxiety disorder often encounters a long-drawn-out sensation of pain or fear and discomfort. This disease may also hurt interactions with friends, family, and peers.

You have a sudden feeling of impending doom, but you can't say what's causing it; your pulse is much quicker, you're shaking, you might be shaking, and you're capable of breathing. This episode continues for a couple of minutes, and then you recover command. You may have just had an anxiety attack.

What are the assaults of anxiety? They're panic attacks, just by a different title. The same symptoms that one encounters during a panic attack are the same signs that one has with an anxiety attack.

They happen without warning and are generally defined as a sudden assault of anxiety and terror that will lead your body to respond as if you were in real damage. Because they're sudden, there's a lot of individuals in public, and this contributes to a spiral of more concern and anxiety over the panic assaults themselves. This concern that one is going to have an assault is probable to lead to another assault. As a result, it's essential that you understand what to do after an episode to minimize your likelihood of recurrence.

Many ordinary people suffer from anxiety, or when they mention, in passing discussion, that they suffer from anxiety regularly. But what's the anxiety about? Anxiety is the word used for various illnesses that can transform into physical disturbances triggered by being tense, nervous, and anxious. There are distinct types of anxiety where you may have moderate anxiety, which may be disruptive to more serious diseases that trigger mental and physical health issues.

Anxiety is often just a normal and safe emotion, but when it begins to impact a person's quality of life and makes things more difficult to do regularly, there is an issue. It is vital for an individual to seek medical help to find appropriate therapy for their situation.

Everyone gets nervous from moment to moment, but when it prevents you from dealing and distracts your regular lives, you're sure to think about having assistance. Anxiety disorder can create you feel highly nervous all the time, even if there is no reason to feel that way. These distressing emotions may be so highly awkward that you can prevent some of the operations that used to be so common and simple for you.

What Are Anxiety Disorders?

Anxiety disorders are situations of people who create intense fear and anxiety for actual or imagined purposes. It has been categorized as a psychiatric science since the last century when it was noted that fear and apprehension could influence the mental and physical tasks of those affected. It manifests itself in multiple diseases that are categorized as mental anxiety, physical stress, and panic attacks. In many cases, anxiety continues even if the perceived danger or feared object is no longer present.

To reply to the query, "What are anxiety disorders," it would assist if its signs were defined as well. It is not unusual for an individual to experience true pain and fear followed by nausea, mistaken thinking, difficulty breathing and shaking, which can last from a few minutes to a few hours. Fear of circumstances, items, individuals or pets is regarded as phobia and is regarded a type of anxiety disorder. Usually this is caused by a poor experience concerning a feared item, condition or creature. For example, the fear of snakes may be triggered by a poor experience involving snakes. Obsession is also regarded a type of anxiety disorder. Obsessive emotions for individuals, items, or situations can trigger an unusual mental malfunction, turning intense obsession into compulsive behavior. Another associated anxiety is anxiety about separation. Excessive connection to an individual can trigger a loss of command when an individual is detached from his loved one. In this scenario, a favorable emotion like affection becomes an abnormality if it is strongly felt for the person. When the beloved is segregated, the activities of the individual concerned become unreasonable. The detachment findings in trauma and the pain it creates are severe.

The classic instance of an anxiety disorder is that when an individual is faced with a constant danger or chance of ruin or illness from job or company, he or she is constantly experiencing prolonged fear for hours or days at a moment. Episodes of this kind are better recognized and defined as panic attacks. In panic attacks, the emotional state starts to influence the physical state, and physical signs such as nervousness, shortness of breath and enhanced heartbeat are experienced by those affected. Anxiety can sometimes take up to six months to become a persistent illness.

Anxiety disorders may also influence kids who suffer from unusual workings of their teaching procedures and social relations when they are afflicted by constant concerns and concerns. They suffer from mental depression, lose their thinking skills, and completely fail in school activities.

Even their physical health is impacted as most impacted kids experience dysfunctions such as diarrhea, stomach upset, enhanced heart rate and blood pressure, nausea, shortness of breath, and many other diseases. Many will eventually benefit from sleeping issues that only worsen their situation. Separation anxiety also influences kids, and the most severe instances of this sort are those concerning kids.

It is essential that easy concerns faced by kids do not become an anxiety disorder. A healthy family atmosphere helps to avoid such stuff from happening. But in case the inevitable occurs, it is always a good idea to get professional guidance and provide therapy for these illnesses. Psychotherapy was the finest remedy when the signs noted confirm that the children's fears belong to the class of anxiety disorders.

The Six Anxiety Disorders

Anxiety generally grows when someone faces something that is out of their comfort zone and can, therefore, be a lot of difficult circumstances. For instance, if you were going to pass an exam, go to an interview or offer a lecture. It impacts individuals in distinct respects because, for some, these circumstances can be deemed ordinary, but for many others, they can impact your whole lives, such as being unable to sleep, making errors at job, or being unable to eat correctly. In particular, anxiety occurs when the response is excessive with what is generally anticipated. Anxiety disorders can be categorized into more particular kinds of disorder. Below are the most prevalent types of anxiety.

Agoraphobia / Panic Disorder

This type of anxiety generally starts with spontaneous panic and develops over time to include fear of distinct experiences such as driving, shopping, going to unknown locations and being alone. A lot of this is trained conduct. For instance, when you are driving, you encounter a panic attack, and riding can cause your anxiety from this stage forward. It's very feasible that the two of them have nothing to do with each other, but the link has been integrated into your brain.

Agoraphobia or adult separation anxiety is a fear of being powerless and alone in the perception of excellent internal risk. This is often articulated as fear of dying, going mad, or losing control of one's conduct. Agoraphobia may contribute to patients staying close to familiar locations and individuals. It could degenerate to the extent of not leaving home.

Specific Phobia

Specific Phobia is a type of situational anxiety, such as fear of flight, fear of heights, fear of insects or snakes, or claustrophobia. It's not just an act of fear; it's real fear that manifests itself in anxiety or panic. Specific or single physicians are situationally linked and can be healed by separating themselves from a case or condition that causes anxiety. However, what at first appears to be specific phobias are, at the root, manifestations of agoraphobia that appear to be various phobias. In other words, you may be suffering from agoraphobia if there are a few activities that make you panic or worry.

Social Phobia

Social Phobia is pathological anxiety manifested specifically as a fear of embarrassment, which may be restricted to public speaking or may be composed of a worldwide shyness that confines social interactions, including dating, marriage, and relationships. People with personal phobia often have poor self-esteem and think that they are not nice enough. These can be kids who have been picked up or who have overprotective relatives. While agoraphobic individuals are scared to be alone, individuals who have personal phobia often tend to be alone.

Generalized Anxiety Disorder

General Anxiety Disorder (GAD) is a sheer concern! General anxiety involves times of severe anxiety and stress. The combined impacts of GAD overtime on the body. People who have a nervous breakdown or a middle-age crisis often suffer from long-term GAD. In general, GAD does not arrive with panic attacks, phobias or pathological timidity. It's the basis of all anxiety disorders, but it doesn't imply you're going to have any of the other diseases. Someone who always seems strained, or is always worried, may suffer from overall anxiety.

Obsessive-Compulsive Disorder

This form of anxiety is generally described by obsessions which are unwanted and intrusive ideas, generally of a brutal or sexual nature. People with obsessive-compulsive disorder (OCD) are trying to rid themselves of these hateful ideas. Short-Term relief from OCD-induced anxiety can be accomplished by participating in compulsions, or ritual senseless behaviors such as saying a phrase over and over, or behavior such as hand washing, inspecting something or going in a certain manner. People with OCD think that their ideas may harm themselves or others. It's not accurate; the ideas are just that, the ideas.

Post-traumatic Stress Disorder

Post-traumatic stress disorder is an anxiety associated with a very stressful or life-changing scenario that someone has just passed through. Some instances may be, whether they are engaged in brutal crime, conflict or fighting, the murder of a loved one, or in a horrible incident. PTSD includes flashbacks that seem so genuine that an individual may think they're experiencing the incident again. Avoidance is an instrument for individuals who have PTSD. For instance, an individual who has been engaged in a plane accident but has been living can prevent flights and aircraft completely.

Not everyone who gets a lot of stress will suffer from PTSD. Everyone's dealing with stress differently. Everyone is experiencing a traumatic event, and the memory and pain of the incident start to disappear after a few months. This is how we're going to be prepared to deal with lives. Can you think that if the grief you feel about losing a loved one was just as strong and as true five years ago? We couldn't live a life like that, but think what? People who have PTSD were living it all those years ago. This considerably disrupts the lives of the sufferer over the years.

All six anxiety disorders are focused around the same fundamental base of pathological anxiety and unusual brain chemistry. Most individuals will be affected by one of these illnesses, but some individuals may experience signs of various illnesses, or their behaviors may alter over the years, and one disease may shift to another illness. While it is essential to know and comprehend what kind of anxiety you may have, it is similarly essential to understand how each disorder operates and how it can influence one another. Go and see your doctor, as always!

<h1 style="text-align:center">Chapter 2</h1>

WHO SUFFERS FROM ANXIETY DISORDER

These fresh results originate from the world's most extensive study of anxiety and depression studies to date, released by scientists at Queensland University.

In two distinct research of anxiety disorders and significant depressive disease (i.e., clinical depression), the writers discovered that clinical anxiety and depression surveys were performed across 91 nations, involving more than 480,000 individuals.

The results, reported in Psychological Medicine, indicate that clinical anxiety and depression are severe health problems around the globe.

Anxiety disorders have been more frequently recorded in Western societies than in non-Western cultures, even those that are presently facing war.

Clinical fear influenced around 10% of the population in North America, Western Europe, and Australia / New

Zealand, as opposed to around 8% in the Middle East and 6% in Asia.

The reverse was true for depression, with individuals in Western countries most likely to be depressed.

Depression has been discovered to be the smallest in North America and the highest in areas of Asia and the Middle East.

Approximately 9 percent of individuals have significant depressions in Asian and Middle Eastern nations, such as India and Afghanistan, opposed to around 4 percent in North and South America, Australia, New Zealand, and East Asian nations, including China, Thailand, and Indonesia.

Alize Ferrari, the lead author of the depression research, claims results suggest that depression appears to be greater in areas of the globe where there is a dispute.

It warns, however, that it may be hard to acquire excellent performance information from some low-and middle-income nations.

"More study is needed on the techniques that we use to diagnose depression and assess its incidence in non-Western nations, as well as more study on how depression happens over a lifetime," she claims.

The lead author of the anxiety research, Amanda Baxter, also called for caution when comparing mental disorders across distinct nations.

"Measuring mental illnesses across societies is difficult, as many variables can affect the recorded incidence of anxiety disorders," states Baxter.

"More study is also required to guarantee that the criteria that we are presently using to diagnose anxiety are appropriate for individuals across cultures." Major depression and anxiety are discovered more frequently in females than in males.

The research also discovered that while clinical depression is prevalent throughout the lifetime, anxiety becomes less prevalent in males and females over the era of 55. About one in 21 individuals (4.7%) will have severe depression at any stage at the moment.

Anxiety— the most prevalent of all psychiatric disorders— currently impacts approximately one in 13 individuals (7.3 percent).

The surveys are the world's most extensive assessments of major depression and anxiety research, the Global Burden of Disease (GBD) study to be published later this year. It will include projections of 220 illnesses, including 11 mental health disorders.

The 2010 GBD Study is the first significant attempt since the initial 1990 GBD Study to carry out a comprehensive systematic evaluation of worldwide information on all illnesses and accidents. Comprehensive and similar estimates of disease burden, injury, and threat variables for 1990 and 2005 with 2010 predictions will be produced.

Women Are Far More Anxious Than Men – Here's The Science

People with anxiety are more probable to skip working days and are less productive. Young individuals with fear are also less probable to join and finish college–translating into fewer life opportunities. Although this proof indicates that anxiety disorders are significant mental health problems, there is inadequate attention provided to them by scientists, clinicians, and policymakers.

Researchers and I at the University of Cambridge wished to figure out who was most influenced by anxiety disorders. To this end, we performed a systematic review of research that revealed the percentage of individuals with anxiety in a multitude of situations around the globe and used strict techniques to maintain the greatest performance of research. Our findings have shown that females are almost twice as probable to suffer from anxiety as males and that individuals residing in Europe and North America are disproportionately impacted.

Why women, huh?

But why are females more probable to encounter anxiety than males do? It could be because of variations in brain chemistry and hormonal changes. Reproductive occurrences throughout a woman's lives are related to hormonal modifications that have been connected to anxiety. Oestrogen and progesterone surges that occur during pregnancy may improve the likelihood of obsessive-compulsive disorder, characterized by disturbing and repetitive ideas, impulses and obsessions that are distressing and debilitating.

But, concerning the biological processes, females and males seem to encounter and respond differently to occurrences in their lives. Women tend to be more susceptible to stress, which can make them more anxious. Also, when confronted with stressful circumstances, males and females tend to use distinct coping approaches.

Women facing life stressors are more probable to ruminate about them, which may boost their anxiety, while males are more probable to participate in effective, problem-oriented coping. Other surveys indicate that females are more probable to encounter physical and mental abuse than males and that violence has been related to the growth of anxiety disorders. Child abuse has been correlated with modifications in brain chemistry and composition, and according to prior studies, females who have suffered sexual abuse may have abnormal blood flow in the hippocampus, a brain region engaged in the treatment of emotions.

The Worried West

Our evaluation has also shown that individuals from North America and Western Europe are more probable to be influenced by anxiety than individuals residing in other areas of the globe. It is not clear what might account for these distinctions. It could be that the criteria and tools that we use to assess anxiety, which has mainly been created for Western communities, may not capture cultural anxieties.

Anxiety could be expressed differently in non-Western societies. For instance, social anxiety in the West is typically expressed as an intense fear of social circumstances, elevated self-consciousness, and fear of being assessed and criticized by others during relationships and achievement circumstances.

However, the strongly associated structure in Asia is Taijin Kyofusho, which manifests itself as constant and irrational fears of causing offense and annoyance to others as a result of presumed private inadequacy. Individuals from other countries may feel too ashamed to show signs of fear that individuals in western societies are comfortable debating—this would imply that the numbers recorded in research on emerging and underdeveloped areas of the globe could be underestimated to the real extent.

Most mental health study has also been conducted in Europe and North America, and very few surveys have looked at anxiety in other areas of the globe. There may indeed be big variations in the burden of anxiety between societies, but further study using stronger techniques of anxiety evaluation is required in this respect.

Either way, we now understand that anxiety disorders are prevalent, expensive, and people with serious human distress. We also understand that females and individuals residing in developed countries seem to have the greatest impact. This knowledge of those who are disproportionately impacted by anxiety can assist guide health service scheduling, delivery, and therapy attempts.

Chapter 3

SIGN AND SYMPTOMS OF ANXIETY DISORDER

Everyone is aware of that sensation of anxiety. Our core begins pounding before we give a large lecture, or when we're going to pass a hard test. We have butterflies in our stomach before the first visit. We're worried about household problems, and we're anxious about requesting the boss for a boost.

Anxiety is an ordinary individual feeling. It's usual to care and think tense or frightened when we're under stress or when confronted with a stressful scenario. However, if those worries or concerns get the manner you want to live your lives, you may have an anxiety disorder. Here, we're talking about indications and effects of anxiety disorders.

Anxiety disorder has a lot of indications. If you have this disease, you might be able to distinguish with most of these indications:

If you're always tense, worried, or on the edge

if your anxiety interferes with your work, school, or family responsibilities,

if you're plagued by fears that you know are irrational, but can't banish

if you think that something poor is going to occur when certain things are not accomplished in a specific way,

if you prevent day-to-day circumstances or event because they create you anxious

if you encounter something sudden and unpredictable.

Anxiety disorders are a set of associated circumstances rather than a specific disease so that they can be distinct from individual to individual. However, despite their many types, all anxiety disorders have one prevalent symptom. They sense constant or serious anxiety or concern in circumstances where most individuals would not think endangered.

Some of the prevalent mental signs of fear are:

- ✓ Feeling apprehension or fear
- ✓ Lack of concentration
- ✓ Feeling worried or nervous

- ✓ Expecting the worst
- ✓ Irritability
- ✓ Restiveness
- ✓ Observing dangers around
- ✓ Feeling disconnected or as if your mind had fallen empty

Anxiety is a result of the body's fight-or-flight response and includes a range of physical diseases. Because of these many diseases, individuals who die from anxiety sometimes confuse their illness with a medical condition.

Here are some prevalent signs of fear:

- ✓ pounding heart
- ✓ sweating
- ✓ upset stomach or dizziness
- ✓ frequent urination or diarrhea
- ✓ shortness of breath
- ✓ tremors
- ✓ muscle tension
- ✓ headache
- ✓ fatigue
- ✓ insomnia

An anxiety attack frequently referred to as a panic attack, is an event of intense panic or dread. It generally happens abruptly and without notice. Sometimes the cause is evident, like being stuck in the elevator. The assault arises out of the box at other moments.

The signs of an anxiety attack are as follows:

- ✓ A rise in overwhelming fear
- ✓ Feeling like you're leaving power or running mad
- ✓ Palpitations of the heart or chest pain
- ✓ Feeling like you want to pass out
- ✓ Difficulty breathing or a choking sensation
- ✓ Hyperventilation
- ✓ Feeling either hot or cold
- ✓ Shaking or trembling
- ✓ Nausea or abdominal cramping
- ✓ Feeling detached or unreal

A lot of individuals face anxiety at some stage in their life.

Anxiety is a very ordinary reaction to stressful lives occurrences such as relocating, altering employment, or experiencing financial difficulties.

However, when the symptoms of anxiety get bigger than the occurrences that caused them and start to mess with your lives, they may be indications of anxiety disorder.

Anxiety disorders can be debilitating, but they can be handled with the appropriate assistance of a medical professional. It's the first move to recognize the indications.

Here are 11 common signs of anxiety disorder, as well as how to decrease anxiety obviously and when to pursue skilled assistance.

1. Excessive Worrying

One of the most prevalent signs of anxiety disorder is overly worrying.

The concern connected with anxiety disorders is disproportionate to the occurrences that cause it and typically happens in reaction to ordinary circumstances To be deemed a marker of generalized anxiety disorder, the concern must happen in most days for at least six months and must be hard to regulate.

It must also be serious and intrusive, rendering it hard to focus and perform regular duties.

People under the era of 65 are at the greatest danger of generalized anxiety disorder, particularly those who are young, have a reduced socioeconomic status, and have many lives stressors.

The excessive regular concern is a characteristic of widespread anxiety disorder, particularly if it is serious enough to interfere with regular lives and lasts almost every day for at least six months.

2. Feeling Agitated

When someone feels anxious, a portion of their sympathetic nervous system is overdriven.

This triggers a cascade of body-wide impacts, such as a rushing pulse, wet palms, shaky hands, and dry mouth.

These signs happen because your brain thinks you are at risk, and your body is ready to respond to the threat.

Your brain sends blood back from your digestive system, and to your organs in event you need to operate or battle. It also raises your heart rate and improves your sensations.

While these impacts would be useful in the event of a real menace, they could be debilitating if the anxiety is all in your brain.

Some study even indicates that individuals with anxiety disorders are not willing to decrease their excitement as rapidly as individuals without anxiety disorders, which implies that they may experience the impacts of anxiety for a larger period.

Rapid heartbeat, breathing, trembling, and dry mouth are all common signs of anxiety. People with anxiety disorders may encounter this sort of arousal for prolonged intervals of time.

3. Restlessness

Restlessness is another prevalent symptom of anxiety, particularly in kids and adolescents.

When someone is experiencing restlessness, they often define it as sensation "on the brink" or getting an "unpleasant desire to move." One research in 128 kids infected with stress illnesses discovered that 74% recorded restlessness as one of their primary signs of depression.

While restlessness does not happen in all individuals with anxiety, it is one of the blue shirts that physicians often search for when creating a diagnosis.

If you encounter restlessness for several days for more than six months, it may be an indication of anxiety disorder.

Restlessness alone is not enough to diagnose an anxiety disorder, but it can be a single symptom, particularly if it happens commonly.

4. Fatigue

Being readily tired is another prospective symptom of generalized anxiety disorder.

Some may find this symptom strange, as anxiety is often linked with hyperactivity or arousal.

For some, fatigue can lead to an anxiety attack, while for others, fatigue can be permanent.

It is not clear whether this fatigue is due to other prevalent signs of anxiety, such as insomnia or muscle tension, or whether it may be linked to the hormonal impacts of acute anxiety.

It is essential to remember, however, that fatigue can also be a marker of depression or other medical circumstances, so fatigue alone is not enough to diagnose an anxiety disorder.

Fatigue can be an indication of an anxiety disorder if it is followed by unnecessary concern. However, other medical illnesses may also be indicated.

5. Difficulty Concentrating

A lot of individuals with anxiety document experiencing trouble focusing.

One research, including 157 kids and adolescents with generalized anxiety disorder, discovered that more than two-thirds of them had trouble focusing.

Further research in 175 adolescents with the same illness discovered that almost 90% indicated experiencing trouble focusing. The worse their anxiety, the more difficulty they had.

Some surveys indicate that anxiety can disrupt operating memory, a sort of brain accountable for keeping short-term data. This may assist clarify the drastic drop in efficiency that individuals often encounter during times of high anxiety.

However, trouble focusing can also be a symptom of other medical circumstances, such as attention deficit disorder or depression, so there is insufficient evidence to diagnose an anxiety disorder.

Difficulty concentration can be a marker of anxiety disorder and is a recorded symptom in the bulk of individuals infected with a generalized anxiety disorder.

6. Irritability

Most individuals with anxiety disorders also encounter extreme irritability.

According to one latest research, including more than 6,000 adolescents, more than 90 percent of those with generalized anxiety disorder recorded sensation extremely irritable during times when their anxiety disorder was at its worst.

Compared with self-reported concerns, youthful and middle-aged people with generalized anxiety disorder recorded more than twice as much irritability in their daily life.

Given that anxiety is connected with elevated arousal and unnecessary concern, it is not strange that irritability is a prevalent symptom.

Most individuals with generalized anxiety disorder study felt extremely irritable, particularly when their anxiety is at its pinnacle.

7. Tense Muscles

Tense muscles on most days of the week are other frequent symptoms of anxiety.

While tense muscles may be prevalent, it is not fully known why they are related to fear.

It is feasible that muscle tension itself may increase emotions of anxiety, but it is also feasible that anxiety may lead to enhanced muscle tension, or that the following variable may cause both.

Interestingly, the treatment of muscle tension with muscle relaxation treatment has been shown to decrease anxiety in individuals with generalized anxiety disorders. Some trials even demonstrate that it is as efficient as cognitive behavioral therapy.

Muscle tension is closely related to anxiety, but the orientation of the connection is not well known. Treatment of muscle tension has been shown to assist decrease the signs of anxiety.

8. Trouble Falling or Staying Asleep

Sleep disturbances are heavily linked to anxiety disorders.

Waking up in the center of the morning and getting difficulty dropping asleep are the two most frequently recorded issues.

Some study indicates that experiencing insomnia during adolescence may even be associated with the development of anxiety earlier in lives.

Research of almost 1,000 kids over 20 years of era discovered that experiencing infancy insomnia was associated with a 60 percent increase in the danger of creating anxiety disorder by 26 years of era.

While insomnia and anxiety are highly related, it is not clear whether insomnia leads to anxiety, whether anxiety leads to insomnia or both.

What is recognized is that insomnia often improves as well when the inherent anxiety disorder is handled.

9. Panic Attacks

A form of anxiety disorder called Panic Disorder is connected with recurrent panic attacks.

Panic attacks generate an acute, overwhelming feeling of dread that can be debilitating.

This severe anxiety is usually followed by rapid heartbeat, breathing, trembling, shortness of breath, tightness of the neck, nausea, and afraid of drowning or leaving power.

Panic attacks can happen in solitude, but if they occur frequently and suddenly, they can be an indication of a panic disorder.

An approximately 22 percent of American adolescents will encounter a panic attack at some stage in their life, but only about 3 percent will encounter it often enough to satisfy the requirements for a panic disorder.

Panic attacks generate highly intense anxiety emotions, followed by unpleasant physical diseases. Recurrent panic attacks may be an indication of panic disorder.

10. Avoiding Social Situations

You may be showing indications of social anxiety disorder if you discover yourself:

feeling nervous or frightened about upcoming personal situations

Worried that you may be assessed or scrutinized by others

Fearful of being ashamed or humiliated in front of others

Avoiding certain personal activities because of these fears

Social anxiety disorder is very prevalent, influencing about 12 percent of American adolescents.

Social anxiety appears to grow soon. About 50 percent of those with it are registered at the era of 11, while 80 percent are registered at the era of 20.

People with social anxiety may look highly nervous and silent in organizations or when they meet fresh individuals. While they may not seem happy on the outside, they experience severe fear and anxiety on the inside.

This aloofness may sometimes create individuals with social anxiety look snobby or stand-off, but the disease is linked with low self-esteem, elevated self-criticism, and depression.

Fear and avoiding personal circumstances may be an indication of social anxiety disorder; one of the most frequently reported anxiety disorders.

11. Irrational Fears

Extreme concerns about particular stuff, such as spiders, confined rooms, or heights, may be an indication of phobia.

Phobia is described as intense anxiety or dread of a particular item or condition. The sensation is serious enough to interfere with your capacity to work usually.

Some prevalent physicians include:

Animal phobias: Fear of specific animals or insects

Phobias of the natural setting: fear of normal occurrences such as hurricanes or earthquakes

Blood-injection-injury phobias: fear of neck, injections, pins, or wounds

Situational phobias: fear of circumstances such as a plane or an elevator trip

Agoraphobia is another phobia that involves at least two of the following fears:

- ✓ Making use of public transportation
- ✓ Staying in open spaces
- ✓ Staying in closed spaces
- ✓ Being in a crowd of people
- ✓ Being home alone

Phobias are affecting 12.5 percent of Americans at some stage in their life. They appear to grow in infancy or adolescent years and are more prevalent in females than males.

Irrational worries that the interruption of regular working may be an indication of a specific phobia. There are many kinds of phobias, but all of them require avoiding conduct and feeling intense apprehension.

If you have had any of these emotions, you show indications and symptoms of fear illnesses. Although this disease can be an incredibly unpleasant and difficult practice, it can readily be handled efficiently. In most instances, cognitive-behavioral treatment, anti-anxiety medicine, or a mixture of both will eliminate your stress or to a stage where it is no longer debilitating.

Chapter 4

CAUSES OF ANXIETY DISORDER

Increasing concerns about job, money, the future, the family, etc. are causing anxiety. Disorder settles in your mind and actions without allowing you feel what's going on, and one day you discover changes in your character and manner of thinking. Even physical symptoms appear, and you're freaking out! Before taking medication, attempt natural anxiety remedies that are secure from any side effects and treat the issue more effectively. Before starting your therapy, it is vital to learn more about how to understand better and have a more effective strategy to heal.

Anxiety is a severe and harmful mental disorder that arises from one's concerns and concerns about the essential problems of one's life. As far as it is within the normal range, you do not need to be worried about it, but if it rises to the extent that you feel uneasy and impacts your ordinary peace of mind and stability, take a practical step to handle it. There are many remedies that can readily assist you in getting out of the situation without having any side effects and visiting your doctor. By taking medications you may feel better at the moment, but because the medications do not contain nutrients and do not match or increase the natural digestion and absorption process, you do not benefit from them as much as you can from natural anxiety remedies.

What causes an anxiety disorder, huh?

There are several variables that can add to an anxiety disorder. An anxiety disorder is triggered by a mixture of several of these variables working together over time. Usually, one factor alone does not cause an anxiety disorder.

Several of the contributing factors are:

Biological Factors

We all have an inborn' fight or flight' reaction intended to safeguard us from damage. When our survival is at risk, the fight or flight response generates physical and psychological modifications that encourage us to behave and defend our survival. These include rapid heartbeat, muscle stress, shallow breathing, and more.

People with anxiety disorders often have a physical overreaction to stress.

This overreaction happens because your body perceives everyday occurrences and circumstances as a threat to survival. In an attempt to safeguard you, your body causes a battle or a flight reaction, even though there is no true risk.

There is some sign that over-reaction to stress is triggered by a chemical imbalance in the brain. However, we don't understand what creates this chemical imbalance at first.

It has not been demonstrated what happens first - the over-reaction to stress that creates the chemical imbalance or the chemical imbalance that triggers the over-reaction to stress.

Can I alter it now? Yes, yes. What is essential to understand is that if you overreact to stress, you can learn to modify it, no matter how it started. You can learn deep breathing techniques, relaxation techniques, and methods such as Anxiety Pyramid (all part of our course) to train your body to respond more calmly.

Stress Overload / Lifestyle Factors

When you experience excessive stress over time, your body can cause a battle or a flight reaction and begin reacting to daily occurrences as if they were a hazard. Poor lifestyle habits, such as overwork, absence of sleep, bad diet, and absence of periodic practice can lead to excessive stress and anxiety.

Let's look at an instance of how stress overloads and lifestyle variables can contribute to anxiety. Donna has been working 70 hours a week for a couple of years. This brings Donna's body under excessive stress. To make matters worse, Donna is so busy at work that she only manages to sleep five or six hours a night, she doesn't practice frequently, and she primarily eats fast food. She can't remember the last time she took her time out.

Do you see how Donna's lifestyle makes her life stressful and generates an adverse snowball effect? Over time, Donna's body begins to see these continual stressors as a threat to her survival. Eventually, her body is "burned out" of repeated unnecessary stress responses. It is in a steady state of alert, contributing to the physical and mental symptoms of anxiety.

Can I alter it now? Yes, yes. You have the authority to decrease or eliminate many stressors in your lives. You do this by incorporating healthy lifestyle habits— by making decisions that encourage calmness, self-care and a balanced lifestyle. Sleep eight hours a night, for instance, instead of six. Eat well-balanced, good food. Work 40-50 hours a week instead of 70 hours and so on.

You can also learn to see stressors less anxiously so that your body does not overreact to stressors when they happen.

Childhood Environment

Your childhood environment impacts the way you believe and behave as an adult. Even though the adults around you meant well, as a kid, you might have discovered the practices and views that add to anxiety.

You might not have been taught, for example, to have a sense of control over your world. You might have been anticipated to accomplish this as a manner of obtaining love and recognition.

You may have been trained to think all or nothing, or you may not have been permitted to convey your emotions or views freely. You might have grown up in an environment that wasn't physically or mentally secure. You may have been often evaluated or criticized. Or maybe you've grown up observing and modeling adults around you who have responded to life in an anxious manner.

Can I alter it now? Yes, yes. No matter what your childhood environment was, you can alter the anxiety-producing patterns of thought and practices that you learned through understanding and exercise.

Thought Patterns

How you believe it impacts how you see the world and how you respond to stress. Negative thinking patterns such as "what-if" thinking, perfectionism, all or nothing thinking, and victim talk can lead to anxiety disorder. In reality, adverse thoughts can cause physical symptoms in your body.

Can I alter it now? Yes, yes. Research demonstrates that you have the authority to alter your mind, which in turn can influence how you feel physically and mentally. Utilizing healthier ideas, you can learn to see the world less anxiously and to feel better.

How do you alter your mind? By using the three "R"s that we discussed in the last newsletter: Recognition, Replace, and Reinforce.

Genetic Factors

Research indicates that panic disorders and obsessive-compulsive disorders tend to occur in households. Although there is some discussion, it seems that part of this family inclination is due to the way you are brought up (environment) and part is due to genetics. There is some sign that genetic factors also contribute to social anxiety.

Although the exact gene has not been recognized, it is thought that genetics play a role in triggering anxiety disorders or at least raising the risk of creating anxiety disorder. Anxiety and genetic disorders, among other factors, are linked to chromosome abnormalities. These findings are confirmed through studies involving twins.

For specific disorders, the connection between anxiety disorders and genetics is better understood. For instance, a mutation of the gene that leads to dysfunction in the brain's chemical systems has been recognized in a panic disorder. Additional possible genetic connections include abnormally enhanced function in some brain receptors; abnormally reduced function in others Chemical imbalances, such as cortisol, associated with stress sensations Impaired carbon dioxide receptors, leading to chronic hyperventilation Obsessive-compulsive disorder has shown a powerful genetic connection with a 45 per cent-65 pe gene impact.

Can I alter it now? No, no. We're not able to alter our genes. It's bad news. Here is excellent news. You can make a positive shift to all the other variables that we discussed that contribute to anxiety.

And, as we stated previously, generally one factor alone does not lead to an anxiety disorder. This is very interesting news! This implies that if you learn how to effectively tackle other variables that add to anxiety, you can overcome your anxiety despite genetic factors.

Medical Causes of Anxiety Disorder

While anxiety can be encountered by anyone, an anxiety disorder for many is related to a significant medical problem. In some instances, an anxiety disorder may be caused by a medical problem. In other instances, anxiety and medical condition may be linked, but an anxiety disorder may not be due to a medical condition.

Potential medical causes include the following:

- ✓ Seizures
- ✓ Diabetes
- ✓ Asthma
- ✓ Heart disease
- ✓ Drug abuse and withdrawal (alcohol and benzodiazepines can trigger anxiety in specific)
- ✓ Thyroid issues (e.g., hypothyroidism or hyperthyroidism)
- ✓ Muscle cramps or spasms
- ✓ Uncommon tumors which produce certain hormones

And many others

While most anxiety disorders evolve in adolescents and young adults, a medical trigger is more probable if an anxiety disorder occurs later in life. Although common, anxiety disorders linked to substance abuse or withdrawal are often undiagnosed. Several drugs can also trigger signs of anxiety disorder.

Anxiety caused by shame Abuse and trauma, including severe loss, is regarded to be the primary causes of anxiety. We may experience anxiety about our finances or a severe medical diagnosis, but most anxiety is shame, which is fear of shame. It is triggered by the painful shame that has been internalized in the past, generally since infancy.

The shame of our anxiety impacts our self-esteem. We're concerned about what we're talking about, how well we're performing, and how others are seeing us. It could make us very susceptible to actual or imagined critique from ourselves or others.

Anxiety may express itself as a personal phobia or in signs of codependence, such as cognitive control, people-pleasure, perfectionism, fear of rejection, or obsession with another individual or addiction. Worrying about our job performance, test, or talking to a community is anxiety about how we're going to be assessed or assessed. While males are more probable to be proud of job losses, females are more concerned about their appearance and relationship. People, in specific, have a shame of anxiety about leaving or trying to be a good supplier. Perfectionism is also an effort to attain an imaginary ideal to be adopted by others.

Chapter 5

ANXIETY AND STRESS

The term "stress" could mean a lot to a lot of individuals. For example, if you were an engineering student, and you were referring to the word "stress," you would be referring to a force sufficient to distort or distort the system. Now here is Webster's definition of stress: the body's particular reaction to stimulus, such as fear or pain, which disturbs or interferes with ordinary psychological balance; physical, mental, or emotional stress or stress. So there you've got it.

Now the "stress" that we're used to hearing about is the "stress" that's capable of generating mood changes, physical diseases, causing addictions, as well as giving you lightning reflexes to get out of the way of a drunk driver, and at the same moment, making it possible for you to enjoy the pleasures of great sex. You see, individuals speak about stress all the time, but few understand a lot about it.

The contemporary use of the term "stress" originated from Canadian endocrinologist Dr. Hans Selye, who referred to stress as the wear and tear of fast-paced living. Dr. Hans

Selye is often called the "dad of stress" because of his studies and findings in this field. Dr. Selye found a familiar sequence of psychological modifications that happen every time individual experiences too much stress or faces challenging difficulties. He called these modifications the "stress reaction," referring to the body's non-specific reaction, to any demands placed on it, whether it is pleasant or unpleasant, whether it is emotional, physical or mental.

In his comprehensive studies, Dr. Selye has shown that the human body reacts with the same distinctive set of modifications to loud noise, sudden temperature drops, viral infections, intense enjoyment, worry, or job problems. Not only the reaction of one organ or portion of the body, the stress response includes a predictable set of physical effects.

Some of the body modifications that accompany stress include symptoms such as increased heart rate, accelerated breathing, mild to heavy sweating, cold hands and feet, and muscular pain. When stress is excessive, intense, and prolonged, it can trigger anxiety and panic attacks.

If you ask ten individuals to give you their definition of stress, it's a nice way to get ten distinct responses. A task that may lead one individual to be stressed out and inundated with anxiety can be seen as a difficult and rewarding job for others. Take something as easy as driving on the freeway, where vehicles zoom in every day. This is a day-to-day occurrence for most individuals who are going to work, but millions are afraid to do it. This journey is considered very stressful for those who don't like quick driving on the freeway.

However, on the other side, take the NASCAR driver, who was born into a family of race-car drivers, and, by the manner, he is well paid to drive very quickly. They enjoy the excitement of going fast... an individual reaction. Mountain climbing, sky diving, speaking in front of a live crowd, taking a challenging test, bungee jumping, or even flying in a plane, would be regarded cool to many, but it could prove to be very stressful to others.

If you ever discover yourself complimenting someone by stating, "Boy, there's not enough cash in the globe to make me take that work," what you're truly doing is recognizing that another individual can do something that you consider stressful, better than you do. And there is nothing wrong with that; because there is no one who can manage every scenario with ease and finesse. You might be able to handle the job, but it wouldn't be what you call a perfect fit. And besides that, who wishes to do something that's totally against their convictions?

There are three phases engaged in the manner we experience stress, the first phase of the stress response, also known as "fighting or flight," is the body's natural response to the perceived threat or true imminent danger. When you cross the street, if you have to avoid an unexpected car, the stress alarm will give you that instant burst of energy you need to get out of the way.

Alarm reactions in mild and sometimes intense forms may add frustration to the person, depending on how they view the scenario. Watching an action-packed boxing game or battling rush hour traffic may generate the same intensity of stress response, but the game results in thrill, while traffic jam can trigger impatience, frustration, and irritation. When you see yourself as a victim of situations and increasingly helpless over the occurrences of your lives, stress can be the end outcome.

If you continue to cause stress through worry and frustration, your body will eventually get into a state of resistance. Resistance is the second phase in the reaction to stress. It's a double-edged sword. It enables you to fight disease and withstand illness. However, repeated or prolonged negative stress can lead to an exhaustion of mental or physical energy and increased susceptibility to disease.

To fuel the resistance phase, the body draws on accessible nutrients and energy-storage reserves. When stress is prolonged, the body forms free radicals, which are unwanted chemicals that have long been involved in degenerative diseases. Free radicals have also been known to accelerate the process of aging. When the body's energy supply is exhausted, the adrenal glands can not deal with stress and chronic anxiety. The second phase of the stress response will, of course, give way to the third phase of exhaustion. The body can replenish its biochemical resources at this point.

As already stated, exhaustion happens in the third stage of the stress response. This state of fatigue persists until the body can attain full rest and replenish itself. Fatigue is the

#1 complaint that has been heard from overstressed patients. In more than 40% of the visits to the physician, patients complain that they are too tired to be at their peak because of pressure. Some of the signs and symptoms of chronic fatigue include fear, tension, anxiety, irritability, temperate outbursts, impaired latest memory, reduced sex drive, insomnia, tiredness, coffee addiction, smoking and stimulants, alcohol and substance abuse, reduced overall health, and happiness.

I want to introduce you to the Four Stress Types of Albrecht. Dr. Karl. Albrecht launched this model in "Stress & the Manager-Make it works for you" in 1979. Albrecht wrote that "most of the chronic stress experienced by Americans in the twentieth century derives from anxiety."

Albrecht recognized four kinds of stress:

1) Time Stress

2) Anticipatory Stress

3) Situational Stress

4) Encounter Stress

I'm wondering how many of these you've encountered?

Time Stress

This is the anxiety triggered by thinking that you're running out of time. There's no doubt that you'll have been in cases where the deadline is approaching. The very fact that time is running out increases your level of anxiety (or pressure).

Efficient time management can overcome this region of stress.

Simple "to do" lists are a nice way to get started. Far too often, we attempt to keep all our duties in our heads. They're jumbled up, and our brains almost feel like they're going to explode! Moreover, when everything is in our head, it's difficult to figure out what's essential or what sequence things should be done in. So, while the "to do" list is very easy, it's also a great way to get everything out of our heads and on paper where we can see it.

The "Urgent / Important" matrix of Steven Covey is an easy-to-use instrument to assist you in prioritizing your job. It allows you to "dig where the diamonds are" but it also allows you to throw away some of the things that are not essential in your work or life.

Time stress is also being compelled on us, as we have more and more duties left on us by others. The best way to counteract this "monkey on the shoulder" syndrome is to increase your assertiveness.

Anticipatory stress

This is anxiety about coming occurrences.

Many of us will have encountered a scenario where we are concerned that "something" will go wrong before a task or event, or that an individual will not like us, or that better work applicants are bound to be there.

For the last 12 years, I've been helping individuals enhance their trust in public speaking.

Time and time again, I've worked with individuals who have a long list of situations that they think might occur. The truth is that most of these fears have never happened. Although there are some fears, if they dwelt on enough, they do come about. If you're constantly thinking that you're going to drop your notes during your lecture, you're going to. This is "The Law of Attraction" which is part of the novel "The Secret." What you are living on is drawn to your lives.

So why don't you instead attract achievement to your career? In secret, Dr. Denis Waitley described the following strong visualization survey: "I took the visualization method from the Apollo program and introduced it to the Olympic program in the 1980s and 1990s. It was called the Visual Motor Rehearsal.

When you visualize it, then you materialize.

Here's an interesting thing about the mind: we took the Olympic athletes and let them run their sport.

There are some other tips for overcoming anticipatory stress: contingency planning is a way of looking at future issues and creating a "Plan B" Just by having that contingency plan, you can overcome stress by understanding that even if there is an issue (and let's face it, they do) you have an action plan, which implies you maintain control of the scenario.

Meditation is a great way to restore your mind and body to the point of calm. Sandra and I are presently following a regular meditation program from Deepak Chopra and Oprah Winfrey (https:/chopracentermeditation.com/) which has had an enormous effect on how we deal with the problems and stresses of our busy lives.

Eventually, sometimes, we need to learn to deal with failure.

I saw a statistic that indicated that the best strikers in the championship scored less than a third of the shots they shot at the objective. They're failures by any statistical measure, but we don't believe they are. They accept that they can't score any time.

Katherine Grainger won Olympic gold in rowing in 2012. But this achievement came after the failure to secure gold at the three past Olympic Games. She just acknowledged that failure sometimes takes place on the path to achievement.

Vincent Lombardi summed it up perfectly: "It's not whether you get knocked down, but whether you get up."

Situational stress

This sort of stress, according to Albrecht, is when we've effectively lost control of a situation. Redundancy, grief, and private conflict tend to fall into this kind of stress.

Just as King Canute tried in vain to stop the sea coming in, we can not always prevent a scenario from occurring. But what we can control is the way we react to the scenario.

If you recall Richard Lazarus ' definition of stress, it's when we're not in command of the situation.

Increased self-awareness enables us to recognize our weaknesses and to be conscious of the triggers that stress us and how we can transform the scenario from a position of weakness to a place of strength.

On a practical level, we can also learn how to handle conflict at the workplace (or maybe it's also outside the workplace).

We often feel that a situation is out of control when a colleague (or likely a boss) is acting aggressively. This aggression, on the verge of harassment, is certainly a reason why some individuals feel stressed at a job. Rather than in Time Stress, learning to become more assertive and less passive will assist in regaining control of the scenario and this specific type of stress.

Encounter Stress

The fourth form of stress recognized by Dr. Karl Albrecht is referred to as "Encounter Stress."

This stress, as the name suggests, revolves around individuals.

Sometimes our relationship with a specific individual or group of individuals is stressful in itself.

This may be because we don't like them-we often hear individuals say that someone always "puts them on edge." Alternatively, stress levels can be increased because the individual you're dealing with is unpredictable. The third reason individuals increase the stress that they are in trouble themselves. Think of individuals working in the health professions. They're dealing with individuals in pain, or maybe they've got to give them some bad news. Either way, the individual being treated will be in some trouble. If you go to a distinct arena, say call centers, you will also discover clients calling in some trouble (usually a complaint, but not always).

The ultimate reason individuals can increase stress rates is merely that you can get to the point of "contact overload." Those of you who are conscious of Myers Brigg's personality kinds may recall that some individuals are "I's." They prefer to think about data before they make choices. If an individual with this sort of character is in a setting with loads of extroverts, he may feel quite overwhelming after a while.

The tips to overcome this sort of stress are comparable to "Situational Stress." Developing your emotional intelligence and self-awareness will be the main strategy.

Extending that self-awareness to knowing how other individuals "tick" becomes a strong instrument. This could be merely by knowing the Myers-Briggs personality kinds or by having a team to have an MBTI evaluation. Learning about the five phases of the grievance is also a helpful instrument. Although this model was initially intended to assist individuals to comprehend bereavement, it is now commonly used to know how individuals cope with trauma in their life.

Symptoms Of Stress

When you have an intense amount of adrenaline in your body, whether it is due to a single event or to the accumulation of occurrences, your bodies become tighter and tighter, and this eventually results in physiological reactions. Heart palpitations, chest, throat and shoulders are always involved-you end up feeling quite slumped and narrow around your throat and shoulders. Your muscles are going to hurt, too.

Whenever you have stress, one of the most prevalent signs is muscle aches, particularly in your legs, your arms. Your body gets tired because your muscles hurt. It's like you've been carrying heavy shopping for a long time, and you can't bring it down. Even after you've slowed down heavy shopping, your muscles still hurt because they've been functioning and tightening up for a very long time.

Your breathing has been impacted. The reason that your breathing changes is because your chest wall is a enormous muscle.

As our bodies grow tighter and tighter, the chest wall becomes like a stiff, stiff fabric sheet. As a consequence, the lungs inside this chest wall no longer have the capacity to grow as they usually do-they only grow a little and therefore do not bring in the amount of water you would usually bring in.

After a while, the brain gives a message to the lungs, "This body requires a little more oxygen. Please breathe a little deeper." Outwardly, you end up sighing. This pushes your chest wall to open up to further development, and that's what the (sighing) reaction is. When you're stressed, you tend to cry more, or you yawn more, because yawning has the same effect. Yawning is when you grab the wind and intentionally push your chest wall to grow.

Again, these are signs of stress.

Other people will notice that they don't sleep well when they're stressed out. Of course it's not. When you're stressed out, your body has a bunch of Adrenaline in it. Adrenalin's aim is to maintain you alert, to maintain you conscious, to maintain you on guard. You're not expected to sleep when you're on guard duties, so when you're stressed, you're not going to be allowed to settle, and you're not going to be allowed to sleep because your brain is thinking and remembering, "Where's the danger?" As your stress rises, you're generating more and more Adrenalin.

The Adrenalin that you are generating is making your brain believe more and more, "Where is the risk?" A nice analogy of this is the meerkat of sentry duties. It's always looking around, checking for risk. This is how the brain is going to become. It believes, "Where is the risk?" And so the Adrenaline that is truly in your body causes your brain to become more alert, more on guard, more worrying. That's why Sensitive people, who always have a bunch of adrenaline in their bodies, tend to be worried. The Adrenalin in their flesh makes their brain believe, "Where is the risk?" And then, of course, the brain starts to believe, "Well, it could be that. It could be that." You're painting what the risk might be, and your body is generating more Adrenalin.

This scenario is turning into an urgent process. The nervous cycle, when it progresses, will eventually trigger your Parasympathetic Nervous System to break down. The Parasympathetic Nervous System is so depleted by attempting to return calm to your body that it no longer works. Now, when you're talking about worrying ideas, your brain is generating Adrenaline even when you're attempting to calm down and you're attempting to inform yourself-your Cortex, "No, no, no, no, there's no risk. It's all right. You're going to get through this. You're a large kid. Other individuals have encountered stuff like this before." That's the way we're talking to ourselves. This is our speak of self-confidence.

However, when your Parasympathetic Nervous System breaks down, even as you try to calm down, you end up generating more and more Adrenaline, and that's when we're under constant stress, and we're no longer able to calm down. That's when we really have a sensation of being traumatized. For the first moment, I'm using the term' trauma'-that's how we feel when we experience the drama of life. We're feeling traumatized. Our body is flooded with Adrenaline, and it truly looks like we're in a car accident, but the vehicle is still moving. We don't understand what the result will be. That's how you can feel when you're traumatized.

At that stage in moment, as well as all the physical responses that your body has, there are other things that are starting to occur. The Autonomous Nervous System begins to fall in the body. The Autonomous Nervous System is a nervous system that is responsible for all tasks over which we have no deliberate power. (It is the Central Nervous System that we can consciously think about. For instance, motion-blinking and walking.) So the Autonomous Nervous System looks after our intestines and digestion, runs after our intestines and removal, looks after our reproductive system. These are all regions of our body which continue to operate without us getting any deliberate power over them.

But when we feel stressed, even a little stressed, what do we begin to realize? We're starting to have stomach upset, and when we have a bunch of stress, these upsets get more pronounced. Some individuals end up with Irritable Intestinal Syndrome or Ulcerative Colitis.

These are quite significant intestinal and intestinal issues. If you're a little depressed or a little anxious, you might have loose stools and need to go to the toilet a lot. But if you have stress over a lengthy span of moment, you will end up with significant intestinal issues and intestinal issues.

Our entire reproductive system may be impacted. It is well recognized that if a female is strained, her menstrual cycle may change. What we now understand, because of the advancement of medical technology, is that people are also very much influenced by stress. With this progress in medical technology and photography, we understand that men's sperm is severely impacted by stress and that men can experience a bunch of unusual sperm and low sperm count due to the interruption of their Autonomous Nervous System.

The other significant components of our Autonomous Nervous System are our Sympathetic and Parasympathetic

Nervous System. These are the regions of our scheme that are responsible for the regeneration and restoration of the body to calm down after stress. And so that breaks down, our body encounters more and more stress without being prepared to recover.

To sum up, when we experience stress, the first thing that begins to occur when our Autonomous Nervous System breaks down is that we have a breakdown of our immune system. We have focused on the Autonomous Nervous System, but the other thing that occurs is that we have a breakdown of our immune system. As we become more strained, we begin to create more colds, flus, bacteria, skin diseases, your eczema-if you suffer from it-may recur. Your Shingles or your Glandular Fever may be back.

How To Differentiate Between Stress And Anxiety

It can be hard to see the distinctions between stress and anxiety from the outside. Both can lead to sleepless nights, exhaustion, excessive anxiety, absence of focus, and irritability. Physical symptoms–such as fast heart pace, muscle tension, and headache–can affect both those experiencing pressure and those diagnosed with anxiety disorders. With symptoms that may appear interchangeable, it may be hard to understand when to operate on deep breathing and when to seek professional assistance.

In brief, stress is the response of your body to a trigger and is usually a short-term experience. Stress may be positive or negative. When stress kicks in and helps you get away from the deadline that you believed was a lost cause, it's positive. When stress causes insomnia, bad concentration, and impaired capacity to do stuff you usually do, it is negative. Stress is the reaction to a threat in any scenario.

Anxiety, on the other side, is a continuous mental health disorder that can be caused by stress. Anxiety does not fade away once the threat is mediated. Anxiety is long-standing and can cause significant impairment in social, occupational, and other important fields of functioning.

1. Stress Is Usually Outcome of External Pressures

The SparkNotes-style variation of the distinction between stress and anxiety is stress is an issue response, and "depression is a stress response," as the American Anxiety and Depression Association reports.

This idea may be a bit complex because individuals who deal with anxiety often deal with outside stressors as well. But you can get a good reading of whether you're experiencing stress or anxiety by getting an honest evaluation of what you're feeling. Are you weary or bored by the stress of coping with the workload of a college, a job assignment, or the expectations of a family? It's likely to be stress. Do you feel a more specific feeling of anxiety or anxiety? Are you more concerned about the future than about the current? Are you worried about something that isn't too tightly linked to your lives, or something unique at all? This is more probable to be anguish. As the UK National Health Service website defines, stress is a "feeling of being under too much mental or emotional pressure," while anxiety is a "feeling of unease, worry or fear." Why this difference is important: stress often comes to an end when the event or responsibility that puts you under stress passes — and so, if you're just stressed, a plan to deal with or deal with the source of stress. As David Spiegel, Associate Chair of Psychiatry and Behavioral Sciences at Stanford University, said, "The main distinction[between the two] is the feeling of helplessness... By drawing your shirts up and tackling that stress, you may feel less relaxed." Stress can often be dealt with in a much more practical way; while anxiety may involve counseling, medication, or other qualified psychotherapists.

2. Anxiety Keeps Hanging After

The Problem Is Resolved None of this is to tell that the real universe has nothing to do with anxiety— far from it. In my profession, some very true job stress has brought to the fore my current anxiety problem. As I tried to deal with this stress, I created a raging case of insomnia along with a good side dish of personal phobia. Then, one day, I was provided a fresh assignment. The problem was resolved. I was supposed to sleep like a dead individual that night, so I was amazed to discover that a whole fresh set of worries kept me up that night, as well as many evenings of my fresh life.

Although it was caused by stress, it was an issue of anxiety. This is not unusual— the National Institute of Health, U.S. National Library of Medicine, says, "Stress is produced by the current stress-causing factor... [while] anxiety is stress that stays after the stressor is gone." So stress can trigger an accident.

Why this difference is essential: yes, anxiety can be caused by stress, but continuous or lasting anxiety needs to be treated as a matter of its own rather than as a consequence of stress. You can't relieve anxiety disorder with a holiday journey or a spa journey (no matter what some less enlightened individuals in your social circle may be telling you). As Spiegel said, "With stress, we understand what we are worried about, but with anxiety, you become less conscious of what you are worried about[at that time], and the response becomes a question of concern."

3. Anxiety Includes Unnecessary Worry Many of the signs of the pressure are comparable to those of anxiety— from sleeping problems and belly problems to irritability and absence of focus— they can look very comparable. There is, however, one revealing symptom that indicates anxiety and only anxiety: a constant sense of apprehension or fear.

According to the National Alliance on Mental Illness, "all anxiety disorders have one thing in common: persistent, exaggerated fear or worry in situations that are not threatening." So, "I'm concerned that if I can't find a new job in the near future, I won't be prepared to afford rent this month," might be a stress-related idea, "I'm worried that my boss will love me secretly and want to shoot me, and that's what I'm afraid of. Some signs remain for an hour or more, "and many individuals go to the emergency room during their first panic assault because they are confident that they have a heart attack or some other lethal health problem — so, yeah, it's a very serious issue.

How I Learned To Overcome Stress

Friends often let me know that my secret is to be secure from stress. I understand what's going on for me. But it didn't come naturally, and at first, it wasn't that simple.

I did all that wrong when I was older. Like many young adults, back then and again, I seemed to be constantly engaged in operations and events that produced the ideal petri dish for increasing stress.

As the old saying goes on, I lit the candle on both ends.

Not only that, but I've also been involved in dangerous activities.

I hung up with dubious friends to add more complex variables.

Of course, because of my bad habits, I had poor self-care.

Over the years, however, I have discovered that I am in command of my conduct and–vitally significant–that my actions have implications.

So, how did I switch from being a true poster child to building stress to learning to live as close to stress-free as possible? Here are the methods that I use to conquer stress. They might be in a situation to work for you.

Stop Attempting To Be The Ideal Man.

I used to believe that I had to be the best in everything I did. I've had to do it better, faster, smarter than anyone else, or it doesn't matter. Part of that was about being a younger sister to a very competitive sibling. Perhaps a portion of that was attempting to please my parents, even though I believe every kid likes it.

The downside to perfection is that a perfection is an elusive object. There will never be an ideal result. Improvement is still feasible, however. What is considered a success today, maybe tomorrow's failure?

My therapist helped me recognize this self-defeating tendency, and he gave me wise advice: you don't have to be perfect. Just do as much as you can.

That sounds simple. But a lot of stress went away when the proposal came down. It wasn't enough to try to do my utmost; it was life-asserting, motivating, and assisting me feel better about myself.

Create A Timetable For This.

When too many conflicting requirements started to permeate my daily life, leading to a drastic uptick in stress, my therapist suggested that I draw up a timetable. I didn't want to do that because I thought the timetables were too narrow. But I agreed to try it out. After all, with the requirements of children and college and work, I required to assist keep everything in order. If the timetable could have done that, I would have been a convert.

To my surprise, setting a timetable helped me develop a breathing room in my life. It reduced some preventable stress and gave me the confidence I required to address other projects. In other words, to position distinct items on my timetable. Everything in a very nice time, of course. I had to get relaxed with my timetable before I started modifying it.

That's the other thing I've found out about scheduling. Like prioritizing duties and setting out a list of objectives, timetables need to be established and adjusted.

It's Okay To Ask For Some Assistance.

I've never liked to ask for assistance. I thought that made me look brittle. But after a few tragedies, traumatic memories, and a lot of heartaches, I gradually discovered that there was nothing wrong with asking for help. If I was ready to assist others in need, asking for assistance when I required it was all right.

In reality, it turned out to be a lifesaver for me to be prepared to ask for assistance from others. There was a moment when I was so desperate that I couldn't understand what to do. My therapist provided some comfort, but I required more. He urged me to speak to my trusted friend, which I did. Just having someone else talk out of judgment was instrumental in increasing the oppressive weight of stress. The truth that we could laugh and do stuff together, like going to a film or having a pizza, assisted us as well.

Today, while I'm not practicing requesting others to assist, if I'm really in need, I'm not going to hesitate to do that. And when they ask for my help, I'm going to be there for others. It's all about being genuine, living up to obligations, wanting to assist when it comes to problems.

Do What You Enjoy To Do About It.

It took me a long time to be able to understand what I did. I came to college at night to get a few degrees, each with a focus on what I believe is my strength: writing. Like millions of people, I had to work in jobs that weren't necessarily gold standards, that didn't fit my objectives and ambitions, but they helped me put food on the table and clothes on my children, cover the lease and cover the vehicle.

I have retained my dream of working in an industry that has enabled me to use my skills. I was lucky enough to work in public relations with a significant automaker, and then become a freelance writer when I retired. It was very helpful to capitalize on my research and my love of writing. Every day has brought fresh problems, fresh possibilities to do what I enjoy.

This is a mystery that I've found out about doing what you're loving. This is going to strike your stress.

Just Create Space For That Game.

Part of the reason individuals get stressed out is that they're working endlessly without a break. Or, the only downtime is when they fall out of bed. Well, I understand that. Well, I've been right there. It doesn't take a genius to recognize that any human being will achieve a point of no return if they fail to add time to rest and recharge in their lives.

I like going to films, man. I also enjoy reading, walking nature paths, landscaping, dining and traveling. Any of these I'm going to find to be playing. And wonders operate to dissipate stress.

After breaking for play — doing what you love for leisure, recreation, or academic pursuit— you can come back to the next item on a timetable, today— do list, or solve an immediate or unforeseeable issue. You have restored harmony and equilibrium to your lives. Stress has no opportunity against a vibrant couple.

Practice Esteem Weekly.

Luckily, I found out how to get rid of stress. In reality, I think that I am very grateful to you. The idea of demonstrating appreciation for all that I have and all that I have encountered is so powerful that I suggest that I do it every day. There's a lot to be thankful for, no matter what your condition or circumstances are. For one thing, you're still alive. You have friends and partners for someone else. You've got another day to gain the favors and donations you're offering today.

No matter what issue you're struggling with, you don't have to cope with it on your own. Talk to someone you trust about what you're going through, and understand that no matter what you're going through, you can begin to feel better.

Chapter 6

BREAKING FREE FROM ANXIETY - REAL LIFE STORIES

Anxiety is just ordinary. Whenever we face a stressful scenario that brings with it the likelihood of a failure or an adverse result, we all feel a little nervous. Anxiety, in reality, is a helpful and useful emotion. It alerts us to risk, keeps us out of harm's manner, guarantees that we are correctly ready for difficulties and encourages us to take action.

However, for individuals with anxiety or illnesses, anxiety is permanent, seemingly uncontrollable, overwhelming, and can become debilitating. It is an unnecessary, unreasonable fear of everyday circumstances and can interfere with regular operations.

Below, we communicated the true-life tales of individuals who have endured anxiety disorder and have begun to live a peaceful and happy life.

Jennifer's Story

It's interesting how stuff sneaks on you. I've been struggling with anxiety for several years now. But I never confessed that to anyone, not even myself. So when I moved to a new neighborhood in Georgetown, I found that I couldn't ride the underground transportation system comfortably because of anxiety –I couldn't get to the Metro. Anxiety kept me above the ground–because everyone at work rode the Metro, it was a simple little symptom that I could point to when asked why I didn't ride it. So I did it. For three years, until I lastly had enough of it.

I went to meet Dr. Kogan at the Center for Integrative Medicine last spring. He was referred to me by a mutual friend, who was also a physicist. Later, I discovered out that she had talked to Dr. Kogan about me in terms of "mild agoraphobia."

The first time I encountered Dr. Kogan, we hardly wasted any time speaking about the Metro. Instead, he questioned a lot of issues about my adolescence, my day-to-day lives, and the amount of moments a day that I experienced anxiety— any fear. Slowly, when I replied his questions, I discovered the reality. Anxiety had been (and had been) influencing me for some moment. In reality, it crept me up and took over my routine.

He introduced me to the emWave system and several techniques including Quick Coherence. At first, I should confess that I was skeptical. I mean, how did this small device assist? Dr. Kogan, however, was kind and patient. He clarified that what he intended to do was to retrain my brain and my thinking habits through meditation and concentration. I promised to practice, but I didn't have a lot of hope.

I would exercise the methods Dr. Kogan instructed me every day. I encountered him every couple of weeks at first, and we'd also exercise in his desk. Then the meetings were extended to monthly visits. Almost without warning, a strange thing started to occur. Suddenly, I started to capture myself, not caring. If you've never suffered from anguish, it doesn't seem like a large deal to you. But believe me when I say you this is a very large deal. Here's an instance of that. As I went to a job (or went anywhere) I used to mentally rehearse what I would do if I stopped working or had a panic attack. Who am I going to call? Where was the closest hospital in town? It's just as exhausting as it sounds.

But after a couple of months with the EmWave, it occurred less and less. And then, one day, it ended.

One day, I was trying to justify it to Dr. Kogan–it was as if my body had chosen not to care about it. Like anxiety and desperation knocked on the gates of my mind, and instead of flinging them open, they remained closed. Dr. Kogan smiled at me when I was done. Well, it was working.

And so we went on — I got better and better with emWave, and ultimately level one and two became too simple, and I focused on three and four. I've been feeling closer and closer. Soon items (crowded buses, poor traffic) that had always created anxieties before they started to appear. Well, yeah.   Not so bad.

Dr. Kogan produced a drastic pronouncement after about six months–he believed I was prepared for the Metro. I had serious doubts about this, but I also trusted him. So I picked up a day, carried along with my natural aid scheme (someone had to hold my hand after all!) and attempted it out. I drove twice, stopping every moment at two stations. After three lengthy years, I went home to the Metro. When we got off, I smiled big, half-anticipated applause from the other passengers–I didn't feel that proud or courageous in a lengthy moment.

The next week, when I went to Dr. Kogan's office, he leapt out of his seat to the press. We were both pleased and came to a fast consensus that while I required to proceed my practice, I had come to the end of my moment with him. He created me pledge to check-in and sent me along the manner with a smile and a hug.

Now, almost a year after that first trip, I'm a distinct individual. Life is not the perfect mind for you. Anxiety is still an occasional visitor to my globe–but (and this is the jerk) it's not a regular guest. And even more importantly, I'm ready to sign up when it does. Dr. Kogan, HearthMath, and EmWave gave me relief from anxiety. But more than that, they've given me my lives back.

Sarah's Story

Since adolescence, I've always been an anxious individual, concerned about stuff rather than playing with other children of my era, but my issues began around 15 years earlier. After losing my greatest friend to cancer and my wife at the moment, abandoning me decades after I had a child, I believed I was handling really well, and then one day I was in town with a colleague, and we were sitting in a bank queue, and we were talking away, and all of a sudden everything came hazily. The only way I can describe it is that it all seemed a distance, and I could see people moving and see their mouths moving, but I couldn't seem to comprehend what they were talking. I can remember my friend shaking me and asking if I was okay and feeling like my heart was about to explode out of my chest and need to find the nearest chair as my legs felt like they couldn't keep me up.

I thought that something was wrong, and I would go as far as to say that I feel like I was dying, and I just required to get back. We left town in a hurry, and my friend cried with fear because she didn't understand what was going on with me. That was my biggest mistake because the only place I felt secure was my house, and it's been my prison for five years. I was compelled to seek medical assistance from my family, and my GP made me feel like I was over. Asking for assistance every moment I required shopping was degrading, and I feel like I was constantly placing my friends and family out. The worst day of my existence went when my girl dropped and hit her wrist, and she was frightened and weeping, and I had to witness someone else take her to the hospital because the panic was too much on me.

My kids used to go and spend the weekends with their dad, and during this moment I also formed monophobia (fear of being left alone) and as quickly as they left home, I would have a panic attack after a panic attack. There's also nothing like watching friends and family go on holiday and knowing that I can't bring my kids anywhere. My oldest child could not have seen me suffering and moved out at 16 to reside with his wife, but my two other kids were my life-savings. They looked after me in a manner that I could never repay. They never questioned me anything, and we spent a lot of hours spending a wonderful time together at home playing matches and observing films. They were the reason that I was determined to heal.

The first stage, the physicians. Endless counseling... going through my past, didn't assist at all. CBT helped in six sessions, but then it stopped and was made to feel a failure because it didn't work. I spent hours and hours browsing the internet and attempting false panic attack remedies and was about to give up when the No Panic connection went up on facebook. I clicked on it, thank God, as I almost didn't, and I would never have been where I am today.

One day when my kids were out, and I was in a hurry, I phoned the No Panic Helpline and spoke to a lady who was the most understanding individual I've been talking to since my panic began. After talking to her a pair of occasions, I was confident enough to join the phone group that she had recommended that I try, and even though I found it hard for the first couple of times, and I don't believe I even spoke apart from my title, it was the best thing I've ever done. I began to see my anxiety in a different light, and I don't say it was instant, but within a year, I was almost panic-free and booked my first vacation. For decades, I've been receiving assistance and guidance almost every day, and I never feel dumb or upset.

I took all the tips I could, and I really listened to what the other individuals were stating in the community, and I carried out a plan that I thought would assist me, and I just attempted my best. I've been panic-free for three years now, and if I can do it, then I can do it to anyone.

Katie's story

I'm not a laid back man. I've never been there. I care, and I get stressed, and sometimes it can be quite negative. This began to get worse slowly last year.

It lasted a long time to realize, but I lost control of how strained I was. I would have randomly started weeping in a taxi on the manner to a party, or I would have struggled to answer the phone at the job because I was scared. I felt like I was losing my mind–my dreams were continually racing, and I kept seeing pictures in my head of death.

Then I had my first SEVERE panic attack one day at the job. Nothing occurred, I was just at my office answering messages, and then unexpectedly I feel like I was losing it. It was like I couldn't deal with anything. I didn't realize I had a panic attack at the moment–all I remember is feeling like I was supposed to die.

With the support of everyone, I arranged an appointment with the GP as well as an appointment with the counseling provider. I've been trained distinct methods and methods to deal with what's going on with me–I've learned about mindfulness, breathing methods, visualization, and the strength of ACCEPTING that you have depression, and that's all right–that's trying to go away. It was very helpful.

I was more in control of how severe the panic attacks were, but it wasn't nice enough for me. So I was starting to feel depressed. I wasn't searching for myself, too. The quantity of alcohol I used to drink every night was huge, even if I was sick during the week. It was self-destructive and not only rendered me sicker, but it also created more mental and private issues. I didn't eat, either, and I rapidly lost a bunch of weight.

I started to feel isolated and disconnected from everything and everything in my career. As a consequence, my self-esteem and trust drifted entirely in the nose. It was a cruel cycle because I felt unable to be alone and said yes to everything–and everything generally meant getting drunk. And I didn't get any self-worth from a job on top of that, as I suffered so much from being sick.

One of my clearest memories of that time was that my oldest, closest friend was ringing and breaking down and saying, "I don't feel guilty." For the first moment that day, I had encountered suicidal thoughts, and I was amazed that thinking about what it would do to my family had no impact on me. Eventually, they'd have to get over it because I can't go on a day longer feeling like this. I think it was the worst day of my life, but I didn't do anything about it, so now I'm taking power out of it.

Going home assisted me in getting a stronger beginning. My mom was mortified at how small I was, and she made it her job to look after me and eat me. Being around the family, too, just reminded me of who I am and that I am appreciated. We sat down and watched the home footage from when I was a little girl, and there was a clip where my dad had to help me with a toy, and I was so upset with myself that I couldn't do it.

I realized then that I'd lost most of my lives to be my toughest critic. I didn't feel the desire to torture my older self for the first moment ever to watch this footage—I felt sad for her. I was empathizing with her, and I enjoyed her. There's nothing wrong with her. There's nothing wrong with me here.

I went back to feeling happy and looking forward to seeing everyone, but I took it easy on the alcohol. I was looking forward to heading back to counseling, too. I had 12 weeks of meetings, and it altered my lives. I've learned things about myself that I haven't realized, and more importantly, I've learned to love myself.

Now, it's nice. Not ideal, man! But that's never supposed to occur, and I can acknowledge it and be all right with it.

I hold a journal of appreciation and write beneficial stuff about it every day.

I'm looking for myself. My anxiety and depression are still very physical, but I stop — I don't force myself to attempt and do anything until I feel better. And I'm sure I'm not going out and drinking.

I don't beat myself up because I have a poor mental health day/week/ moment.

I'm doing more for myself. I'm no longer trying to be all stuff to all individuals. Nothing bad is going to happen if I'm not a perfect person, and if someone doesn't want to be in my lives, that's their loss.

It's been a hard couple of years, but I can honestly say that I'm a very lucky individual, and I'm not ashamed to say that

I'm a very lucky individual who sometimes suffers from anxiety and depression. It's not me all the time, and it doesn't describe me. When someone gets sick or injured, they're still the same person.

Look after yourself and be patient, kind and unjudgmental to others.

Vennie's story

I was in the middle of my gym practice, doing my bench presses on the sloping barbell rack. There was severe pain in the center of the collection on the left side of my shoulder. Stirred, I thoroughly placed the bar in the metal brackets and waited, attempting to get a feeling of what was going on. When I got up, I felt light-headed, as if I had come up too rapidly, and the wind had sucked out of my head. Putting my hand on the table that I folded over to keep equilibrium. I pushed my palms against my chest, attempting to find the pain, and I saw that I was pulling a muscle. I looked at a clock on the far wall, at a fixed point, and I noticed the second side tick. After about a minute, the sensation disappeared, so I settled back down and kept going.

The pain returned by my third rep, more constant, more challenging. It was followed by this tingling feeling that began at the fingertips of my left side and went up to my arm like a foreboding signal that squirrels through my flesh. I placed the bar down again, and I sat down. It's not ordinary, I believed. I took a sip of water and waited for it to happen again. This moment, though, fear had started to bubble, that I was attempting to speak out of myself. If I don't know, it's not there. But it was creeping quickly, though. Then it's quicker. Then, when I got up again, it was on me.

My heart picked up the pace, rocketed forward, and beat furiously, like someone slamming at the accelerator. I verified my heart rate on my watch monitor—150 bpm per minute, considerably greater than usual, despite the reality that it was my ordinary exercise. Something about seeing the figures, the acceptance of the truth, made me hesitate. I started to hyperventilate, and space started to rotate, the perimeter lights exacerbating the impact.

I've got to get back, I believed. If I create it home — see Nicole — I'm going to be ok. I cried out for sunlight and fresh air, but the chaos of the outside world rendered it worse. My body feels like a bitch, and I had to drag myself through the parking lot. I discovered my vehicle, scrambled to get my keys out and the unexpectedly hard job of opening the gate. I let gravity knock me to the driver's seat, and I took a glance at myself in the mirror, attempting to balance that picture with that individual. I seemed to be a stranger to myself, far from my legs, swimming, and disoriented. When I attempted to turn the vehicle around, it feels like I was intoxicated. I wasn't able to match my motions with the vehicle, and I pushed the vehicle directly back to the sidewalk. After having to park back and get out, I discovered a bench in front of the strip mall to wait for it all out. There was nothing balanced. The red mailbox on the sidewalk seemed to be flipped on its side. The wooden bench wasn't constant at all. Everything was in motion.

I don't want to die; I ask myself.

My heart rate read 170 bpm on the table. But my energy level was running out of me, like a liquid, my arms were heavy, and my body was starting to sink. It's like the pressure is growing from my fingers to my throat, and then to my head. The floor is coming up to reach me, at an angle, like I'm trying to move through.

I scrambled for my mobile and dial 911 and went down to the sidewalk; my arm hooked around the street sign pole.

"I have a heart attack," I said as soon as I heard someone's button responding. I couldn't define it in any other manner, and I understand it's going to break through with those phrases. The tinny voice of a youthful woman attempted to calm me down. "Okay, remain there. We're supposed to submit some assistance. Where are you now?"I am in the shopping center of York and the Seminary. In front of the Rite Aid, "I said. "I'm on the sidewalk. "Okay, somebody's on the manner. Stay there and drink nothing. "Her voice was a slender noise from a remote planet.

"Please speed up," I asked. "I can't do that much longer." She began to wonder what I had done and what I had done. I've been trying to breathe a lot less conversation. I was trying to imagine every breath passing through me. My ears were as heavy as if I had been alive for days. My mouth was dry, and my body was fainting, like water flowing out of a tire.

I feel caught inside my own body, like a ship in a tailspin, in the direction of the world. I shut my eyes and said a prayer: Lord God, kindly let me do this.

Allow me to lift my children to see the next day.

Please pardon my wrongdoings and build a smooth heart in me. I beg that you will be done in the mighty name of Jesus, Amen.

The next morning, I left the gym and only half a cup of coffee, hoping to remove the nightmare of the day before. But it was back late in the afternoon. Well, Creeping and then on me. I've been captured in another assault. It went on again that night. The next morning, then.

Then the next one.

Then the next one.

My body has been in a full-blown uprising. Anxiety began to spread outward, like water pursuing splits and splits. I began to doubt it all, never feeling grounded or secure. My sleepy neighborhood has become a minefield of triggers. As days turned into weeks, I became too scared to sleep, too paralyzed to do anything. I was caught inside the walls of a prison of my own.

This was the series: my heart would begin punching tough, and then quickly and quickly. My eyes would go dry, and then I would begin to feel tired, like the ground was curving upwards, or I could feel the spin of the world. A feeling would begin to creep up my left side: fingertips, hand, velocity, and strength up my arm and left side.

Then I would have had chest pain and trouble breathing that generally spiraled into hyperventilation. It was a powerful force I couldn't see that was smothering me. It was like I was at the bottom of a deep hole, and the earth was filling up above me.

My own body had become unreliable, and the globe was risky. Nicole attempted her utmost to soothe me, but she was as mysterious as I was. Watching me obsessively check my heart rate, or seeing me get up in the center of the night to move to the ER, she feels trapped. It was difficult for her to watch this weakened guy, afraid to be home by himself, always seeking confirmation that he would be all right. I was the shell of a man she had grown up to know and love, as needy as our child's son.

Things are getting worse and worse. After waking up too many times in the center of the night, I began to sleep in my vehicle at the hospital parking lot in the event of an assault. I refused to go anywhere that wasn't a fast trip to an emergency room. Walls have gone up all around me. I was frightened by the loss of command, the failure to predict, the fear of never feeling normal again. I refused to ride lengthy distances, and I was scared to work out at the gym, hoping that I'd maintain it at bay. But I still had customers that I needed to train. I left and postponed a couple of meetings until I had to get back to the job. I was secretly scared to do even the fundamental cardio or lift that I had my customers do. The thing that I had once come to for peace and power was frightening to me now. I've often invented in-juries or other reasons why I couldn't engage. I would have been a fraud, a show to my lives.

Sometimes when I call 911, an ambulance would arrive and dissipate as soon as the paramedics approached me or I went to the hospital. It just disappeared after I picked up the 911 phone. The appearance, the proposal, would negate his need for assistance. This was the first to think that all of this was from a greater well.

At the ER, I would be hooked up to the IV, and I would be given a sedative to attempt to cause sleep. Then there were numerous blood tests, CT scans and ECG's, leaving me with no responses. After every visit, the ER doctor would say, "Follow your primary," but I didn't have one. About a month after the attacks, I was back at the ER when they gave me a Lorazepam pill. It was like a refreshing wind that was flowing through my body. It was a comfort to me. It was magic, man.

I lastly went to see a general practitioner the next morning; I was off for typical insurance purposes. Dr. Barnes was a big white man in his early thirties, with one of those big buildings that showed you he was heavy once. He wore slender screen lenses and had silver hair on his sides— a bald road down the middle — and a shortened beard.

Dr. Barnes stared at all my blood work, exams, and medical records from all the emergency room trips, a virtual stack of data. I cycled through the description of the symptoms again, which I wanted to do because it was like unlocking the trap. The aura of fear flowed into space just by telling me some of those phrases.

During my recitation of tales and symptoms, he sliced me off and put his hand up. "Okay, Quentin," he said in a nasal tone. "It seems to me that you have a serious anxiety disorder." "An illness?"I questioned, confused. "You mean like some dis-ease?"Yes. This is very prevalent. It's called Generalized Anxiety and Panic Disorder. "I informed him about the Lorazepam I got from the hospital, and he gave it to me every day. I scarcely took medicine as a kid and vividly remembered my mother's reluctance to medicate me as a teenager at the psychiatrist's office. She knew much more about the hazards associated with it than the average person because she had been med-certified and worked in the industry for 25 years.

There was a cultural divide, as well. There wasn't a single child in my society on drugs for conduct. One of my brothers was hyperactive, and he was the only child I knew who got the medicine to calm down. I understood some diabetics, but that was it. No one's taken anything for anything.

But what was the decision I had? I was a drowning guy, and the doctor carried me in a ship. I placed my full confidence in my doctor's hands, happy to learn that my issue had a title and that the symptoms were treatable.

"How soon am I supposed to carry this?"I questioned, looking down at the prescription sheet. A weird combination of happiness and distrust weaved through me. "Well, the disease is quite serious," he said. "Medication is the only effective way to control your anxiety." He didn't answer my question, but I didn't press it. I was pleased to have a weapon to fight back.

Anna's story

Although many individuals may feel nervous from moment to moment, individuals with a generalized anxiety disorder (GAD) discover that everyday concerns hurt their lives.

Mother of Three Anna Vaught shares her 35-year experience of coping with fear–how she handles it and balances her mental health with getting a good profession and being a mother.

Early signs of anxiety Family members have always regarded Anna, a nervous kid. At college, she was concerned about individuals dying, professors in specific, and had a feeling of intense fear with palpitations and wet palms.

When I was highly nervous, I just wanted to run and hide from everybody for no obvious reason. I'd remain up all night weeping.' These emotions were still going on in her adolescent years. During her GCSE examinations, she would have sudden, overwhelming emotions of panic, such as heart palpitations and fear of fainting or sickness.

I went to see my GP, but I just said that I was ill so that note could go to the exam board to clarify my achievement on the paper.' For families who are worried about their kid during the exam session, there are methods to keep them under stress.

Anna, however, did not realize that her anxiety could be treated and kept her as hidden as much as possible from her friends and family. Because I internalized my emotions of anxiety, I began to feel self-harm that I believed would give relief from the overwhelming panic.' Her anxiety persisted at the university and increased in her first year of death, followed by her mom passing away after graduation.

Seeking Anxiety Treatment It wasn't until mid-twenties that Anna received the assistance she required. After a serious episode of depression that co-existed with her anxiety, she opened up to her GP.

She was delighted when she learned that her emotions of hopelessness and depression were related to an anxiety disorder. Various medicines were provided, including four distinct kinds of antidepressant medication. None of them worked for Anna; while they helped a lot of individuals, the medication rendered her tired and unable to work well during the day.

Anna also rejected Cognitive Behavioral Therapy (CBT), a therapy that attempts to alter the way you believe and act. I didn't think that this was correct for me, as I would pick up the treatment shortly after I received it and go back to being nervous,' she says.

It was then that Anna's doctor proposed CAT (Cognitive Analytic Therapy), a therapy that utilizes certain components of CBT while searching at the root causes of anxiety and behavioral patterns. CAT altered Anna's lives–after years of anxiety, she lastly thought that this could assist her cope.

Living with anxiety and anxiety attacks Despite studying how to deal, anxiety can still sometimes influence Anna. For example, she might misinterpret someone's look and overthink the meaning of it, often for a few days.

The critical voice in Anna's head reminds her of the uneasy personal scenario of the past that will form the way she interacts in the future. This could affect her relationships, as she is constantly analyzing discussions.

Anna has, however, developed ways to deal with anxiety attacks. If she feels surrounded by fear, she's going to imagine her emotions as a "train of anxiety." I'm not going to start the train off the line,' tells Anna. I'm rushing along the train and sitting with the feeling.' Anna was motivated by her capacity to handle her anxiety. There are activities I'd like to do in my career, but I've felt kept away because of my anxiety,' she says. I think that I can do what I want to do now, realizing that I have coping processes if I begin to feel uncomfortable.' When she became a mom, Anna recognized the significance of maintaining her anxiety under control. She thinks it's essential to be accessible to your family if you have or believe you may have a mental health problem. Anna is talking publicly with her spouse and three kids to see that mental health can be achieved.

Anna's advice on dealing with anxiety Anxiety is a perfectly rational response to several things, but when it becomes irrational, make sure you find your coping strategy." If you're anxious about the everyday situation, try to imagine the worst possible scenario, and realize it's not the end of the world if it happens." Although this is something that you may have to deal with occasionally, realize it's just a blip, and you're going to have a good time, too." I always say to myself, don't bring today's emotions tomorrow. Tomorrow is another day." Over the years, I have created a feeling of humor that enables me cope with the situation.'

Chapter 7

HOW TO GET RID OF ANXIETY - USE YOUR FEAR BEFORE IT USES YOU

Getting rid of anxiety disorders isn't the same thing as carrying out garbage. If you bring your garbage out to the sidewalk, it's gone indefinitely, and it's not coming back. But when you attempt to get rid of acute anxiety, you often discover that this job is more like a child's "Whack a Mole" match than it's like getting out the garbage. Each moment you hit a mole, more moles will pop up. Every attempt you create to battle anxiety encourages you to do more.

You need to be willing to operate intelligent, not difficult, to conquer anxiety disorders. This manual is going to assist you to do this.

One of the greatest ways to know how to combat anxiety is to know how to raise fear. It's not that prosperous individuals are never scared; it's that they're more scared of not having a complete, wealthy existence than they are of anything else that might hold them away. Instead of being paralyzed by fear and anxiety, they use fear to move them further toward their objectives. Here are some recommendations from Tony to assist you to move your anxiety back to higher success:

1. Use The Rocking Chair Test

Stimulated by a hard choice? Some types of anxiety are situational, meaning that they arise from a certain case and go away once the issue is settled. It's not a question of how to combat anxiety in these instances. Instead, it's about how to make a healthy choice rapidly. Try using a Rocking Chair Test, one of Tony's indecision-related techniques of coping with anxiety. The Rocking Chair Test is easy: take time and think of yourself at the age of 85. You're in your rocking chair, reflecting on how you lived. Imagine your lives if you did whatever it was that made you nervous or fearful; maybe it's changing professions, learning to fly a helicopter, or going on a fresh journey. How do you think about it? What did your lives look like as a consequence of the choice?

Now, proceed to imagine yourself later in life, and this moment, examine how your life appears without attaining the thing that gets you nervous or frightened. This is the route where your worries are dominating you. Do you look back and feel like you lost it? Have you any apologies or sorrow? Do you want to make distinct decisions? Compare the emotions of both opportunities and use that emotion to create your decision. After this workout, one way or the other, you will feel faith in your choice.

2. Find Something Even More Frightening

If your worries keep you from having exceptional life, it's time to learn how to get rid of anxiety. Once you become more fearful of not getting action, you feel less daunting about what concerns you. Be more afraid to settle for less; be afraid to live a life that is far below what you receive or want. Don't allow your fear to keep you back. Instead, believe of it as a factor that drives you to do the stuff you want in life. It may be hard, but challenge yourself to move past the concerns that hold you back and encourage you to be more scared of not attaining your objectives.

This is a change in thinking that not only helps you learn how to overcome anxiety, but also helps you develop empowering views that transform negatives into positive ones. If you recognize that your concerns–whether true or imagined–are less frightening than striking your goal, you will be motivated to behave.

3. Dance With Your Anxiety

For some individuals, it's not feasible or even important to get rid of anxiety. If you can use the energy of anxiety and fear to move forward, you can transform anxiety into a beneficial thing. Remember, you don't need to feel nice about being efficient. Tony taught himself to say, "I can be scared, and I can do it anyway. I don't have to get rid of fear; I have to dance with it. "While you may never understand how to get over anxiety entirely, you can acquire the understanding and abilities you need to move forward when you think that you're caught up in times of anxiety-related fear or panic. When you train your brain to accept that you're scared but still move forward, it doesn't matter if you're scared— you have a freedom that most people don't have.

Anxiety doesn't need to be a restriction. It can function as a variable, instead, to move you forward. Instead of approaching an "I'm so worried" mantra condition, you can turn that nervous negativity into beneficial energy by teaching yourself to adopt rather than run away from whatever causes your anxiety.

4. Change Your Physical State

Those who have suffered anxieties understand that they can rapidly spiral out of control, leaving you shaking, sweating, or discovering it hard to breathe. Feeling internally nervous has a major impact on your physical being. How can you fight it and get rid of your anxiety? The response might be as easy as altering your physical state. Raise your chest a little bigger, get up and dance, or go for a stroll. Most of us are looking for something incorrect in our globe. If we search for what's incorrect, we're always going to discover it. But there's a lot of what's correct in the globe, too. Changing your physical state implies altering your concentrate and, as Tony suggests, where the focus is, energy flows. An easy shift of landscapes or an increase in your heart rate can often be enough to offer you the ease you need to know how to combat anxiety.

5. Use The 90-Second Rule

When you experience stress and want to get rid of anxiety, follow the 90-second rule of Tony. If you're never expecting to feel nervous or scared again, you're going to be disappointed. To some extent, everyone experiences fear or anxiety. You can't alter the reality that life's stressful times occur, but you can decide to move past them and regulate your feelings. The next moment you feel nervous, use the 90-second rule. The 90-second law is one of Tony Robbin's normal anxiety remedies. Accept that you feel scared at the moment and look at a timer or clock; you've got 90 seconds to feel awful.

Align your head and your soul through the sucking of your core, feel your problem for 90 seconds, find it out, and then alter your concentrate and let it go. Allow yourself 90 seconds to feel pity or fear or rage or concern. But once those 90 seconds are up, it's time to move forward and accept that those feelings are in the past. Continue to work towards your objective regardless of your feelings. Once you've done this enough times, you'll discover that getting rid of anxiety will make it simpler for you to accept the emotions instead of keeping them back.

6. Strengthen Your Support System

Who you spend time with has an enormous effect on your mind and how you cope with your feelings. If you have a good connection and helpful colleagues, you are much more inclined to cope well with stress and keep a favorable perspective on life. But even if you have a nice assistance scheme, you can always reinforce it. If you want to discover methods to overcome your anxiety, consider collaborating with a wellness coach. Not only can a coach help you find the grounds for your anxiety and assist you in getting rid of anxiety for good, but they can also assist you create practices and values that will boost your satisfaction in all fields of existence.

Don't beat yourself up to feel nervous about it. Everyone experiences anxiety at some stage in their life and the objective is to manage it effectively so that it does not badly affect your happiness. Recognize that although fear may be component of your tale, and you may never find out how to overcome anxiety, you still have the power and drive you need to succeed.

9 Ways To Get Rid Of Anxiety In 5 Minutes Or Less

Approximately 40 million people in the U.S. have an anxiety disorder, ranging from generalized anxiety disorder (GAD) defined as "intense concern you can't regulate" to panic assaults, with heart palpitations, trembling, shaking, and sweating.

Whether you encounter moderate or intense anxiety, there are measures you can take instantly to calm down and soothe yourself. Here are some of the best ones:

1. Stand up straight

According to Tamar Chansky, Ph.D., psychiatrist, and writer of Freeing Yourself from Anxiety, "When we are nervous, we defend our upper body— where our hearts and lungs are located — by hunching over." For instant relief from stress, sit up, draw your knees back, place your toes uniformly and extensively apart, and open your chest. Then take a deep breath. This posture, coupled with deep breathing, enables your body to understand that it's not in risk right now and that it's in command (not powerless). If you can't stand up (i.e. if you're in your vehicle), fold your knees back and open your chest. The most significant thing to do is avoid hunching and breathing profoundly.

2. Play 5-5-5 game

When you're nervous, you're often captured in an (adverse) thinking loop. Play this to get back to your body and quickly prevent your fear: look around and identify five stuff you can see.

List 5 sounds that you can hear.

Move five components of your body that you can feel (i.e., rotate your ankle, wiggle your legs, shake your head up and down).

It may sound stupid, but it operates.

3. Lavender oil Sniff

Lavender oil has several healing characteristics. It encourages a sensation of calm and encourages profound, restful sleep. It could even assist with headaches.

Keep a bottle of lavender oil at your office (or in your wallet if you have one) to assist decrease your anxiety. Breathe it in and rub it into your temples when you need a peace boost. Bonus notes to combine sniffing with profound, even breathing.

4. Look at a funny video, yes.

Watching a video of your favorite comedian or blooper reel will assist you to avoid feeling nervous. Why is that? Because at the same time, physiologically, you can't giggle and remain nervous. After a laugh, your body relaxes in a manner that gets rid of anxieties. Plus, according to the Mayo Clinic, laughter draws in oxygen-rich air that stimulates your body and lungs and stimulates your endorphins.

5. Going for a quick walk

 Exercise is a long-established way to reduce anxiety. Concerning boosting your amount of feeling-good neurotransmitters, a quick walk clears your mind and makes you breathe more deeply again - and anxiety is closely related to shallow breathing.

Studies also indicate that individuals who practice strongly periodically are 25% less probable to create an anxiety illness.

6. Accept your anxiety

This may sound counterintuitive, but Chansky suggests that admitting your anxiety (instead of feeling embarrassed or frustrated) will truly help you feel less nervous.

It doesn't matter whether you've acquired your anxiety from your family or lifestyle or both. It's here now, and you recognize that instead of battling it, you're free to know how to handle it. Accepting this doesn't imply giving up, either. It implies you avoid using energy to bet on yourself for being nervous and instead discover what works for you when it goes to self-confidence.

7. Listen to the most pleasant song in the world

This song was designed specifically to calm your nervous system down. Anxiety was discovered to be reduced by up to 65%. Here's a loop that you play on repetition.

8. Re-label what's going on here.

If you have a panic attack, and your heart is racing, it's simple to think something like, "I'm going to die." Instead of purchasing this incorrect idea, re-label it. Remember, "This is a panic attack. I've had them before, and they don't kill me; they're going to happen. It's going to happen, too, and there's nothing I need to do." In actuality, panic attacks are an activation of the body's fight-or-flight response that doesn't kill you — it holds you alive.

9. Do anything.

Do anything. Clear a couple of stuff off your office. Walk to the kitchenette and have a glass of water. Walk outside and find a flower to smell— it doesn't matter. Doing an intervention interrupts your thinking pattern, which is often where anxiety begins.

When it goes to preventing anxiety, self-sustaining is effectively a deep act of self-love.

Chapter 8

PROVEN NATURAL REMEDIES TO CURE ANXIETY

If signs of anxiety interfere with your regular lives, consider these trusted lifestyle modifications that have proven to be natural anxiety cures.

Drink Chamomile Tea

Why: Chamomile compounds may relieve signs of general anxiety disorder, according to tiny research released in Phytomedicine in 2016. It states that "oral consumption of pharmaceutical-grade chamomile is secure, with few moderate side effects that are statistically and clinically indistinguishable from placebo." Even better, the research describes that there were no indications of side effects such as weight gain that may happen with some traditionally prescribed anti-anxiety drugs. However, as is prevalent with research on alternative and natural therapies, scientists clarify that more research requires to be undertaken to further explore its advantages. Still, it can't help to drink some chamomile tea; while you're at it, here are more methods to use tea for what's wrong with you.

Get Your Daily Dose Of Omega-3s

There is proof that omega-3 fatty acids may relieve stress. A systematic review and meta-analysis released in JAMA Network Open in 2018 evaluated the prospective advantages of omega-3 polyunsaturated fatty acids (PUFAs) for anxiety. Although its writers mention that more clinical trials should be performed, their data is'... the first meta-analytical proof, to our understanding, that omega-3 PUFA therapy may be connected with fear decrease.' Canned fatty fish, such as tuna and salmon, walnuts and linseeds, are all major sources of omega-3 fatty acids. If you're not a tuna fan, here's some omega3-rich food for people who don't like fish.

Breathe In Lavender

You've likely heard of lavender oil as one of many natural remedies to decrease anxiety. But is that efficient? A 2016 issue of The Mental Health Clinician reports that vital lavender oil has a "favorable security and effectiveness profile." Accordingly, the journal notes that it is "a sensible option to consider in clients with anxiety disorders." Try to place a few bottles of lavender essential oil in your pillow or toilet or add a few drops to a cup of boiling water and inhale for a Qu.

Add L-Lysine to your diet

L-Lysine is an amino acid, and one of the construction blocks of your brain's chemical messenger called a neurotransmitter. Some lower trials have related L-lysine to a decrease in signs of anxiety, including one in Biomedical Research. It was discovered that a mixture of L-lysine and L-arginine was "a possibly helpful nutritional action in otherwise healthy people with elevated subjective concentrations of emotional stress and anxiety." Protein-rich foods such as red meat, seafood, and cheese comprise L-lysine. If you like cheese, then you're going to want to learn about the six most healthy types of cheese you can consume.

Get Some Sunlight

Head outdoors to naturally boost your vitamin D concentrations and reduce your anxiety. Doing so may be a natural way to calm down, according to the 2018 problem of Behavioral Sciences. The writers of the journal have drawn on an increasing amount of research trying to connect natural, indoor settings to stress decrease. In the end, they found that a wide range of study points to a positive association between the two. They do, however, render it apparent that several factors can guide the experience. For instance, private emotions about nature, differences of opinion about what makes the natural environment attractive, and other mental health circumstances are just a few factors.

Combat Stress With Exercise

Keep moving to assist in decreasing your anxiety. After all, the Anxiety and Depression Association of America says that even short walks of about 10 minutes may stimulate the mood. It makes sense; practice generates endorphins, chemicals that are natural painkillers to your body. In turn, you're better prepared to sleep, which can reduce stress. Exercise can also enhance general cognitive function and decrease fatigue. If you believe you'd rather watch the grass develop than enter the gym, bring this advice into account to learn to love exercise.

Take A Hot Bath

With Epsom Salts First, the warm shower is always soothing. Second, adding some Epsom salts to the water may assist in increasing your mood. These salts comprise magnesium sulfate, which may have an anxiety-fighting effect. For example, information published in the 2017 issue of the journal, Nutrients, notes that"... there is suggestive but inconclusive evidence of a beneficial effect of magnesium supplementation in mild anxiety." As is the case with a lot of research on natural remedies, this one also points to the need for further investigation.

Cut Out (or Down) Caffeine

You're likely going to have your coffee maker or local coffee every morning. However, if you are struggling with anxiety, you might want to re-evaluate your caffeine habit. The Mayo Clinic states that caffeine can contribute to sleep issues that affect mood and, in turn, may worsen depression. Anxiety and depression often happen together, the hospital contributes, stating that "caffeine can make anxiety worse." Therefore, attempt natural anxiety remedies, such as chamomile tea, or attempt your water intake —make sure you eat water in the correct manner.

Avoid these foods

Caffeine, tobacco, and sugars. The Mayo Clinic says that, for instance, liquor and caffeine can make anxiety worse.

Magnesium, vitamin B12, and zinc deficiencies have been related to signs of anxiety disorders. Vegans and vegetarians in specific should be aware of their B12 consumption, as vitamins can only be discovered in animal products.

Studies connect the dissatisfied intestine with the dissatisfied mind, so prevent eating products that are hard to digest, such as processed foods, ingredients elevated in saturated fats, and fried foods. Instead, the Mayo Clinic indicates healthier alternatives, such as fruits, fish, and vegetables.

Finally, don't let yourself get so hungry that your blood sugar falls, which can contribute to an anxiety attack.

Eat These Foods

Healthy foods Clean food range in wooden boxes: fruit, vegetables, vegetables, superfood, cereals, leaf vegetables on gray concrete background A healthy diet and a reduced level of anxiety seem to go hand-in-hand. Harvard Medical School's information relates to something called "dietary psychology." In other words, your brain reacts to the food you consume. This might influence your mood. Cut down (or remove) high-sugar diets and processed foods.

Here are some good suggestions: blueberries and peaches contain nutrients that alleviate stress and have a soothing impact.

Whole grains are wealthy in magnesium and tryptophan, an amino acid which your body transforms to serotonin. Serotonin is considered to calm down and to enhance your mood.

Oats also boost serotonin output and are strong in fiber, which helps avoid blood sugar peaks that influence your mood.

Avocados, eggs, milk, and meat are all filled with B vitamins that can assist in avoiding anxiety.

Foods that assist control and reduce the stress hormone cortisol include vegetables wealthy in vitamin C, such as oranges, omega-3 fatty acids, and magnesium-rich products such as spinach and other dark leafy greens. Indulge in dark chocolate every once in a while, which also helps reduce cortisol.

Chapter 9

UNDERSTANDING DEPRESSION

I think that the word "depression" has come to be used very casually and generically. The mental countries that used to be merely "mood changes," "boredom," "solitude," and "sorrow" have now been blown up to become "depression." While ordinary individuals have begun to believe that they are suffering from "Psychological Disease," many individuals with severe pathological "Depression" are being treated very lightly and are not supplied with appropriate social support and therapy services. Either way, the impact is a matter of interest.

WHO claims, "Depression can be long-lasting or recurrent, significantly impairing an individual's capacity to function at a job or college, or to deal with regular life. At its most serious, depression can contribute to suicide."

Understanding DEPRESSION, in its true context, places moral responsibility on us-NO THE WORD CASUALLY FOR EVERY FEELING OF SADNESS, GUILT, LOSS,

FRUSTRATION, IRRITABILITY ETC. in us or our close and dear ones.

It's common to feel small or low at some stage in a person's lives. Depression, however, is a completely distinct question, as it is a disease that impacts the whole individual, that is, the mood, the mind, and the body. It affects everything from the manner an individual lives and sleeps to the manner they care about themselves and believe about stuff.

Depression or depressive disorder is very distinct from an easy sensation that it is small. It is not an indication that an individual has a fragile personality or a situation that can be desired. People with this disorder can't just switch off and think lighter. If someone has a depressive disorder and does not pursue suitable treatment, their symptoms may last for weeks, months, or even years. Getting the correct treatment for depressive disorder can help most people who have depression.

Here's what the American Psychiatric Association is telling us— the assassination of a loved one, the loss of a job, or the end of a relationship, are difficult circumstances for a person to conquer. It is prevalent for a sensation of sadness or grief to develop in response to such stressful conditions. But the SADNESS and the DEPRESSION is not the same thing. While feelings of sadness decline over time, depression can continue for months, even years.

Depression is the most prevalent issue of mental health in the United States of America. It impacts 17 million people of all ages, groups, races, and backgrounds each year. Depression is a severe illness, and everyone needs to understand whether you're suffering from depression, or have a buddy or loved one who's suffering from depression, or whether you're just learning about it. Even if you don't have a disease or understand someone who's suffering from it, it's still a good idea to get acquainted with it so that you can acknowledge its signs at any stage in moment, get a diagnosis right away, and get the assistance you or your wife or loved one wants.

The key to handling and overcoming depression at the time lies in its early diagnosis. If you are willing to recognize its indications in time and have treatment, you can easily overcome it.

What's depression?

Depression should not be confused for the usual feeling of a bad mood, sadness, or feeling down. Such emotions are ordinary responses to everyday occurrences and are often overcome within a short time.

If someone is depressed or has mood swings for weeks, months, or longer, and prevents an individual from doing his or her regular operations, that might be depression.

Types Of Depression

Other types of depression or subsets of the disease may be caused by particular circumstances.

Major depressive disorder

It is projected that 16.2 million adolescents in the United States, or 6.7% of adolescents in the United States, had at least one significant depressive event per year.

Persistent depressive disorder

You may have a single episode of severe depression, or you may have recurrent periods of depression. Persistent depressive disorder or dysthymia is a chronic low-level depression that is less serious than major depression and lasts two or more years. These continuing emotions of profound sorrow and hopelessness, as well as other signs such as poor electricity and indecision, happen in 1.5% of U.S. adults in a specified year. Women are more common than males, and half of all instances are deemed severe.

Bipolar disorder

Another form of anxiety is bipolar illness or manic-depressive disorder, which affects about 2.8% of the U.S. inhabitants in a specified year. It happens similarly in males and females, while 83% of instances are deemed severe.

The disease involves the development of manic or energized mood. They can sometimes be preceded or accompanied by episodes of depression. The existence of these episodes determines the sort of bipolar disorder diagnosed.

Seasonal depression

If you have a significant seasonal depressive disorder, also recognized as a seasonal affective disorder, your mood is influenced by seasonal change. Up to 5% of the U.S.

population has a situation in a specified year. Seasonal depression is typically caused by the beginning of autumn and extends throughout the winter, usually occurring in summer and spring.

Geography and distance from the equator have a significant role to perform in this disease. Women are also four out of five individuals with a disease.

Postpartum depression

As many as 80% of fresh mothers experience "child blues" and signs include mood swings, sorrow, and tiredness. Usually, this kind of feeling happens within a week or two.

This is due to hormonal modifications following childbirth, absence of sleep, and the pressure to take care of a fresh child. If these signs continue for more than a few weeks and the severity rises, this may be an indication of major depressive disorder with peripartum start, also recognized as postpartum depression.

Other symptoms include withdrawal, loss of appetite, and negative thinking. According to the American Psychological Association, between 10% and 15% of U.S.

women have a depressive disorder within three months of birth. One in five new females encounters minor depressive incidents, and as many as 10% of new relatives may experience this scenario as well.

Dr. Christina Hibbert, the award-winning author, and clinical psychologist, call this "family disease." Untreated, it can be dangerous to households and children.

Psychotic depression

When major depression or bipolar disorder is preceded by hallucination, illusion, or anxiety, it is referred to as major depressive disorder with diagnosed features. Approximately 25% of individuals admitted to the hospital due to fear have psychotic signs.

Who Suffers From Depression

Depression can influence anyone, irrespective of era, culture, family history, or gender. The causes of depression are wide-ranging and can be caused by a variety of variables or occurrences in a person's lives. Sometimes depression doesn't have a cause or a trigger. While depression may have an impact on anyone, it may have a different impact on some individuals or demographics. Depression demographic studies have shown that: women: women are twice as probable to die from depression as males; women may be at greater danger of depression partially owing to hormonal modifications caused by puberty, menstruation, menopause, and pregnancy (Depression.com, 2009) Women are twice as probable to die from anxiety or phobias as males and when anxiety is present (Depression.com, 2009). Some of the world's most famous and influential rulers have endured depression, including Winston Churchill, Abraham Lincoln, and Mahatma Gandhi.

Men:

Although females are more probable to have depression, males are more probable to undertake suicide–and this may be because males are more unwilling to seek assistance with anxiety (NHS, 2009); people are more probable to use alcohol or substance abuse to cover their disease, and many will be undiagnosed.

Children:

Depression can influence individuals of any era, including kids; studies have shown that 2 percent of adolescents in the United Kingdom are influenced by fear (NHS, 2009); approximately 1 in 10 kids under the era of 15 have a mental health disorder, such as depression. The distinction between females and children is less than the distinction between adult males and females (Overcome Depression, 2009); the incidence of mental health circumstances continues to boost in adolescence.

Elderly:

Older individuals may lose loved ones and have to adapt to their own life. They may be physically sick and unable to be as effective as they once were. These modifications can all lead to depression (Depression.com, 2009); many older individuals are not influenced by depression and are not seeking assistance with their situation; about 1 in 5 elderly individuals in the society are suffering from depression, while 2 in 5 in the care centers are struggling with depression (Overcome Depression, 2009).

Why Do Women Suffer More From Depression?

Women are twice as probable to encounter major depression as males do. They are also up to three times more likely to die from anxiety disorders or to try to commit suicide. The reasons for these gender differences are not clear, and some belief these statistics to be insufficient because women are more "vulnerable" and therefore more likely to report these diseases. On the other hand, several remarks tend to check the legitimacy of these disparities, such as the past half-dozen.

1. Hormonal variations are generally referred to as the main reason for this. Women are confronted with a lot more hormonal modifications than males, which are connected to signs of depression. Up to 15% of customers experience postpartum stress in premenstrual dysphoric illness. Depression is so prevalent during menopause that involutionary melancholy was a well-defined psychiatric diagnosis until 1980. Women are also more likely to benefit from hypothyroidism, which is often linked to depression.

2. Women have a complicated genetic susceptibility to depression compared to males who rely on identical and fraternal twin studies, as well as documented and comprehensive family history documents.

3. Women tend to be more engaged in private interactions than males and last longer when they are interrupted. More married females and homemakers have increasingly joined the workforce and have discovered it hard to juggle work and family duties, such as caring for the elderly. Significant European studies in more than 30 nations, with a total population of 514 million, have lately revealed that depression in middle-aged females has increased in 40 years due to these stresses. Women between the ages of 25 and 40 were three to four times more probable than males to be depressed.

4. Women live longer than men, and serious ancient age is often linked with bereavement, loneliness, bad physical health, and other factors predisposing to depression.

5. Women are more probable than males to consult a physician if they do not feel well or have signs of depression and are therefore more probable to have a diagnosis. There is also some proof that both masculine and female physicians are more likely to diagnose depression in females than males with the same problems.

6. Seasonal Affective Disorder (SAD) is four times more prevalent in females than males, and its incidence is rising as far away as you are from Ecuador. For example, Tromso, a city in Norway 200 miles north of the Arctic Circle, has nearly 50 days of winter when the sun is never seen. This period is referred to as market den (Murky Time) and, as one psychiatrist said, "The whole town is slowing down, people's concentration and job abilities are lowered, and they are always exhausted. There is a noticeable rise in depression, especially among females. Sleep pills, tranquilizers, and pep pills are growing significantly, as crash. The return of the sun after seven millennia is a lab.

Chapter 10

SIGN, SYMPTOMS, AND CAUSES OF DEPRESSION

Depression can be a very debilitating disease and is frequently ignored as a minor illness. There are many elements of life that are affected by depression, including personal life, working lives, and well-being. A lot of individuals attempt to say someone who's struggling with depression just to shake it off or push your way to do something. However, things aren't that easy when you're dealing with clinical depression. At some stage in everyone's lives, depression is going to happen, but clinical depression is a lot distinct, and it's something that remains with you through your lives. It can be difficult for individuals who do not have clinical depression to know precisely what the individual is going through.

One of the easiest methods to diagnose depression is by looking at its signs and symptoms. Generally, individuals seem to realize that depression is a disease in which an individual has poor spirits, lacks interest in job, is unable to focus, and suffers from a pessimistic approach. In brief, a depressed individual lacks the passion and vigor of life.

However, the key to identifying depression as the real cause is to concentrate on the duration of the moment and all prevalent signs. If you feel stressed and if your depression lasts longer than a few weeks, depression is more probable to be liable. To assist make a correct diagnosis, it is also necessary to determine whether you are suffering from multiple indications and symptoms of depression, including:

- ✓ Loss of interest in day to day regular activities
- ✓ Always sad
- ✓ Insomnia
- ✓ Feeling difficulty while focusing
- ✓ Difficulty in creating choices and disturbed cognitive behavior
- ✓ Unintended loss or gain of weight
- ✓ Bad temper
- ✓ Restiveness
- ✓ Feeling tired or very weak
- ✓ Feeling insignificant
- ✓ The Loss of Sex Interest

✓ Thinking of suicide

Mysterious physical issues such as body aches and pains

Signs and symptoms of depression may occur at any age, and any stage of life. But depression is found to be more prevalent in both older adults and women. Ironically, it is often seen in recent times that even adolescents are suffering from this disease.

Teenagers are confronted with a host of pressures. Teenagers often tend to be moody, a symptom that is very common at this age. As a result, it makes it a little more difficult to understand their depression. People in depression are withdrawing from society and appear to be sad. Alternatively, in teen depression, the usual reaction to depression is aggression, rage, irritability.

Some of the signs of adolescent depression include:

✓ Hopelessness or sadness
✓ Irritability, rage, or unfriendliness
✓ Crying regularly
✓ Retreat from friends and family
✓ Changes to eating and sleeping routines

- ✓ Restlessness and nervousness
- ✓ Feelings of lack of value and guilt
- ✓ Lack of excitement and lack of motive
- ✓ lack of energy or fatigue
- ✓ Striving to concentrate
- ✓ Thinking of suicide

If your teen suffers from severe adolescent depression, see your doctor. The path to the retrieval of your depressed teenager may be bumpy, so be careful. Please be compassionate to your kid. A healing touch, a loving hug, kind phrases are going a long way to making your kid feel pleased and come out of depression.

Apart from the signs and symptoms of depression mentioned above, there are many other explanations for depression. They are close death, detachment, denial of affection, stress, anxiety, unfulfilled requirements and wishes of existence, etc. Long-term physical illness or some chronic disease also contributes to depression. But there is a wide distinction between "feeling depressed" and suffering from clinical depression. Signs and symptoms differ from individual to individual and may increase and decrease in severity over moment.

Some of the clinical signs of anxiety are:

- ✓ Unhappiness and unending sadness
- ✓ Lethargy
- ✓ Inability to appreciate the beauty of life
- ✓ Sudden Appetite Change
- ✓ Disruption in ordinary sleep pattern
- ✓ Feeling low on trust and self-esteem
- ✓ Moving about sluggishly
- ✓ Moving around slowly

Depression is a disaster in our lives if left untreated. In reality, our professional and private lives can be interrupted. It is essential to note that if signs and symptoms of depression remain for more than a few weeks, medical action is needed.

CAUSES OF DEPRESSION

There are always upheavals in human minds in a globe troubled by wars and disputes, plagued by ignorance and disease. Frustrations, conflicts, anxieties, and emotional pressure open the door to depression. The causes of depression cannot generally be linked to a single reason-in reality, and it is the culmination of several distinct triggers that cause depression. Depression is not just a state of mind-many occasions; the imbalance in chemicals in the human body (called neurotransmitters that carry signals in the body and bones) also creates depression.

Some of the triggers of depression are as follows:

Genetics

As with many other health illnesses, heredity performs a part in depression. Not everyone with depressive signs has a family history of emotional problems; nor does getting depression in your family ensure that you will experience depression. However, study has shown that people with mental illness in their context are more likely to experience signs of depression themselves.

Trauma & Stress

Trauma and stressful life activities, such as loss of a loved one, abuse, acute disease or suffering, or moving to an unknown place, may cause depression in some people. These occurrences lead in modifications in the level of neurotransmitters (addressed in more detail subsequently), leading to imbalances in brain chemistry that trigger signs of depression.

Medications & Recreational Drugs

There are a big amount of drugs that many of us regularly use that can trigger depression in some individuals. Prescription drugs, birth control pills, anti-inflammatory drugs (including steroids), antihistamines, cholesterol tablets, elevated blood pressure medicines, antidepressants, and tranquilizers are all related to depressive signs. Nicotine, caffeine, liquor, and street drugs are all known to cause depression in some people as well.

Neurotransmitter Imbalances & Abnormalities In Brain Physiology

Neurotransmitters are chemical "messers" in the body that control mood, thought, and memory. If neurotransmitters are not accessible at adequate concentrations, depression may lead.

Researchers have observed that people with depression often have an abnormally tiny hippocampus, a small brain construct strongly connected with memory. A narrower hippocampus has fewer serotonin receptors; serotonin is a neurotransmitter that is essential to the regulation of feelings.

Brain Inflammation

Inflammation, often associated with autoimmune disorders such as diabetes, causes a reaction of the body's immune system. Regulatory proteins called cytokines are used to control probable infections; these peptides generate a stress response, changing the concentrations of certain neurotransmitters, resulting in depressive signs.

Toxicity

Environmental toxins, such as heavy metals and molds, may cause an immune response that triggers a cytokine response.

Digestive Disorders

Digestive dysfunction, including intestinal diseases, bacterial overgrowth, gluten, and other food allergies, and decreased protein digestion, may also cause an immune system response that may lead to depression.

Nutritional Imbalances

Many important nutrients, especially B vitamins, minerals such as zinc and magnesium, and Omega 3 fatty acids, are building blocks for important neurotransmitters. Insufficient dietary intake of these nutrients can contribute to imbalances in the neurotransmitter, a significant cause of signs of depression.

Impaired Methylation

Methylation, a metabolic process that occurs in every cell in the body, is essential for the production of hormones, for the regulation of neurotransmitters, and for the synchronization of neural networks that influence mood and cognition. If this method is disabled, the entire scheme may be disrupted.

Hormone Imbalances

When hormones such as insulin, thyroid or adrenal hormone, and sex hormones are not accessible at the appropriate concentrations, they may badly influence the manner we believe and feel.

Chapter 11

HOW DEPRESSION AFFECTS YOUR LIFE

Have you ever noticed why some individuals are the victims of depression while others are not? Maybe someone near you is showing indications of depression, maybe you've been infected with it, or maybe you think like you might be depressed. They prompt one to wonder: why does depression happen? What are the causes of depression, huh?

Depression is a highly complicated and multifaceted mental illness. There is no single clear source of depression; it may happen for a variety of purposes. For some, depression can grow as a serious medical condition owing to their genetics and family history. Others acquire depression as a consequence of modifications in lives, such as family issues, relocating to another location, or the death of a loved one. One thing is certain; some individuals are biologically susceptible and are more probable to create depression than others.

There are certain life occurrences and conditions that improve the likelihood of getting depression or render an individual more susceptible to depression in subsequent lives. Some individuals are depressed because they are or have been victims of physical, mental or sexual violence in the past. Depression is also sometimes the outcome of private conflict and disputes with relatives or loved ones. Another life activity that causes depression in many is the murder or loss of a loved one. Sorrow and mental unrest encountered during this era are probable to raise the danger of depression.

Other significant life events that could boost the probability of emerging depression are getting fired from work, experiencing financial difficulties, or getting married. The stress and anxiety that emanates during stressful life activities are what predisposes an individual to depression.

It is essential to note, however, that depression does not happen as an "ordinary" response to nervous or hectic life occurrences. You might be asking, "A lot of individuals are going through such life occurrences every day, and they're willing to cope with the stress just perfectly. So why is the stress of this life case influencing me / my friend / my family member to the stage of depression?"Even if you or someone you understand is suffering from a milder type of depression, this disease may influence many facets of your lives. Depression interferes with a person's sexual wishes, job, and college achievement, and sleep and eating practices. Depression even causes individuals to experience physical pain regularly, such as headache and back pain.

Depression is going to affect everything you do in your daily lives. It is not feasible to recover rapidly and easily from depression as well as from cold or stomach pain. Many of us with depression create the error of assuming they're just feeling sad, and they're going to go back with moment on their own. Even if it does for some, but for millions of others, depression is a constant experience that doesn't go away. Think about it this way; feeling down is a fleeting emotion, while depression is a continuous fight with oneself. Slowly, it chips away at your mental, emotional, and even physical power until you start to feel tired and desperate about life.

Depression impacts our manner of thinking, our perspective on life, and our behavior with friends and family. Depression can make you disinterested in college, practice, or even hobbies and events that you used to enjoy. Depression helps you withdraw from culture, making you feel weary and weak. Concentrating or concentrating on anything becomes difficult, negatively affecting your productivity. You'll realize that you're either sleeping too much or too little, eating too much or too little. Even fundamental day-to-day activities, such as brushing your hair or teeth, or having a shower, seem tough and exhausting and almost impossible to do. People who suffer from depression are also more susceptible to other physical and psychological diseases.

Don't forget that depression doesn't only impact the lives of those who suffer from it–depression impacts everyone around them, like family members, friends, and co-workers.

It is, therefore abundantly evident that depression functions as a figurative monster to ruin your lives. Depression leads an individual to become progressively alienated from community. Depression impacts one's private and academic life, as well as one's career. People are losing their employment, their family, and sometimes even their loved ones. Their research and careers are significantly affected, sometimes forever.

It's important to know as much about the complications of depression as possible so that we don't let it go untreated. If we overlook depression or fail to seek assistance, we run the danger of further complicating and ruining our private and professional life. It is essential that we seek assistance for depression, not just to save our employment and friendships, but also for our own sake. That's the only way to combat a monster called depression, and not let it eat your whole lives.

And, most important to remember, depression isn't more strong than you are. Your power is higher, and you can battle depression and conquer depression. The best you can do for yourself when you're a victim of depression is to seek assistance. Reach friends and relatives, pursue the assistance of a specialist, and communicate it and recognize it to yourself. Confronting it and seeking assistance is the only way to stop an adversary called depression from taking your lives.

Chapter 12

HOW TO NEVER BECOME DEPRESSED: PREVENTION

In a large-scale study called The National College Health Survey, about 45 percent of college pupils report being depressed year after year to the extent that it is hard to operate and 80 percent claim they are frustrated.

Depression does not discriminate between old and young. The average age for the start of the depression in the 1960s was 29. The average age for the start of depression is now 14.

Depression is an issue that wants to be resolved. Luckily, there is more and more study to suggest that it can be, and without the use of psychiatric drugs.

There are many lifestyle modifications and stress management methods that can be used to prevent or deter depression. There are some causes that could lead us to experience depressive episodes. While causes may be distinct for everyone, these are some of the finest methods you can use to prevent or avoid a relapse of depression.

Exercise Regularly

Practicing frequently is one of the greatest stuff you can do to improve your mental health. According to the Mayo Clinic, training can assist in the therapy and avoidance of depression in several important ways: it improves your body's temperature, which can have a calming impact on the central nervous system.

It produces chemicals like endorphins that can increase mood.

It decreases immune system chemicals that may make depression worse.

All kinds of physical exercise can assist cure depression, but it's important to activity frequently. You can: join a sports team or a workshop (like yoga or kickboxing) where you will be component of a group as well as being involved.

Take the steps instead of the lift.

Make it a practice: this is the best way to preserve the fitness standard that is most efficient at stopping depression.

Learn more about practice, depression, and brain » Cut back to social media time. Research has shown Trusted Source that enhanced use of social media can trigger or lead to depression and poor self-esteem. Social media can be addictive, and there's a need to remain linked to relatives, friends, and even coworkers. This is how we schedule and invite each other to activities and share big news.

However, restricting social media time can assist avoid depression from occurring. You can do this by deleting all social applications from your phone using web-blocking extensions that only allow you to use certain locations for a preset quantity of time, going to social media for a fee, and avoiding logging on multiple occasions a day to do something.

Build Strong Relationships

It is vital for our mental health to have a strong support system and an efficient private life. Research has shown that even "suitable" social support can protect against depression.

Make sure you link to friends and family periodically, even when your life is busy. Attending social events when you can, and finding new hobbies that can help you meet new people can help you build new relationships.

Minimize Your Daily Choices

Have you ever walked into a theme park and been struck first by what you want to do? Researchers think that too many choices can efficiently cause major stress that can add to depression.

Psychologist Barry Schwartz, the writer of the novel "The Paradox of Choice," discusses studies that demonstrate that when confronted with too many decisions, those who strive to create the greatest possible choice—"maximizers "— are confronted with greater levels of anxiety.

For many of us, our lives are full of choices. What clothes do we wear and should we purchase yogurt or eggs or bagels or English muffins or sausages for breakfast? The pressure to make the right — or wrong — the choice is believed to add to anxiety.

Learn To Be Decisive More Quickly.

Reduce the choices you will have to create during the job week: plan your dresses and prepare your dishes and get ready to go.

Reduce Stress

Chronic stress is one of the most prevalent triggers of depression that can be avoided. Learning how to handle and deal with stress is crucial for ideal mental health.

To handle stress, you can:

avoid chronic stress which one of the most preventable prevalent triggers of depression.

Learning how to handle and deal with stress is crucial for ideal mental health.

You can: avoid over-committing to stuff to managing stress.

Practice your mindfulness or meditation.

Learn to let go of things you can't regulate.

Maintain Your Treatment Plan

If you've already experienced one depressive episode, there's a decent chance you'll experience. This is why keeping your therapy schedule is so essential.

This includes: continuing prescribed drugs and never abruptly preventing them from having "maintenance" meetings with your therapist every so often when remission is consistently exercising policies and coping processes that your therapist has taught you.

Get A Lot Of Sleep.

A lot of high-quality sleep is needed for both mental and physical health. According to the National Sleep Foundation, individuals with insomnia have a 10-fold danger of emerging depression relative to those who sleep well.

To get better sleep, you can:

Do not look at any of the displays for two hours before bed (including your phone!)

Meditation before going to bed

Avoid caffeine afternoon

Stay Away From Toxic Individuals

We've all met that person who makes us feel bad about ourselves. Sometimes they're an outright Tyran, and sometimes they gently placed us down to create themselves feel easier. They could even be someone who takes benefit of us. Toxic individuals should be prevented at all expenses, irrespective of the particular scenario. They might reduce our self-esteem.

One research in 2012 discovered that adverse social interactions were related to greater concentrations of two proteins recognized as cytokines. These two proteins are related to both inflammation and depression.

To prevent individuals from being toxic, you should:

Stay away from anyone that makes you feel worse about yourself.

Cut the individuals out of your lives who are taking advantage of you.

You know the indications. If someone spreads rumors or talks badly about someone as soon as they leave the room, they're probably going to do the same for you.

Eat Well

A recent study has shown that taking a high-fat diet regularly can have comparable impacts as chronic depression pressure. An unhealthful diet may also deprive your body of the essential nutrients it requires to keep physical and mental health.

Obesity can contribute to bad self-esteem, especially when you start adding to other people's assessments and assessments. According to the Centers for Disease Control and Prevention, there is a powerful correlation between obesity and depression. National research found that 43% of teenagers with fear were obese. Adolescents with depression were more likely to be obese than those without depression.

If you practice commonly, get enough sleep and eat well, you should have a nice weight on the spot.

Manage Chronic Conditions

People with other chronic circumstances are at a greater danger of developing depression. Chronic circumstances are not something that can be prevented, but in many instances, they can be handled.

You should:

Consult your doctor if your disease or symptoms are getting worse.

Follow the therapy scheme thoroughly.

Take your medicines and create adjustments to your lifestyle as suggested.

Read Prescription Medication Side Effects Carefully

However, a variety of distinct prescription drugs may trigger depression as a side effect. Read the tags thoroughly before carrying them. You can speak to your doctor and see if any other drugs or procedures can fix your depression-free situation as a side effect.

- ✓ Some drugs that may trigger depression include:
- ✓ hormonal medications, like birth control pills
- ✓ beta-blockers
- ✓ corticosteroids

✓ anticonvulsants

Reduce Alcohol And Drug Use

Excessive use of alcohol and any drug use is correlated not only with greater risk of depression but also with elevated risk of relapse of depression. Limit the consumption of alcohol and eliminate any use of drugs as securely as feasible.

Because alcohol restriction can be difficult in certain personal conditions, you can: order an appetizer instead of a beverage at a happy hour.

Plan and invite your colleagues to activities where alcohol is not essential.

Order cranberry juice; you don't have to inform anyone that there's no vodka in it.

Get Off Nicotine

Smoking and depression can perpetuate each other, although any nicotine can function as a cause for depression.

To stop smoking, you can: focus on your reason to quit, and remind yourself of this every moment you're tempted.

Know what to expect in advance of the moment.

Tell your colleagues, and invite them to assist keep you responsible.

Quit at the same moment as your buddy.

Plan For Unavoidable Known Triggers

There are some causes of depression, but if you learn about them, you can prepare for them. And that could assist you in dealing with it preemptively. Examples of inevitable depression causes could be the centenary of your child's suicide or divorce, or knowing that you'll see your ex and their fresh spouse at college.

To schedule for these causes, you can:

understand that it's coming up, and understand what it's going to mean to have plans with a colleague, or invite someone to check in with you to remind yourself that you're going to get through it.

If you're worried, you can also create an appointment with your therapist for more advice to assist handle it ahead of the moment.

Chapter 13

HOW TO GET RID OF DEPRESSION

It is often more difficult for us to enjoy our lives and be satisfied with the current state of things and the things around us. Thinking that we're not happy with this or that comes into our lives, creating the feeling that everything is wrong, and there's no way to fix the issue if any. This is the state of depression, and in such a scenario it is essential not to let these emotions develop and grow stronger. Below you can discover methods and means to get rid of depression and appreciate your lives.

Best Depression Treatment Options

Doctor Visit

Check for medical conditions; if present, treat them. If you believe you may be suffering from depression, a nice first step is to consult a physician who can create a favorable diagnosis and refer you to a psychiatrist or a psychologist. The doctor may also determine whether the causes of depression may have originated in some other, potentially undiagnosed, physical illness; sleep apnea, diabetes, thyroid diseases, and Parkinson's disease are just a few of the diseases that can replicate or contribute to depression. Premenstrual dysphoric disease (PMDD) and occurrence of menopause are other prospective causes of depression in females. If your diseases have a physical or hormonal root, the fundamental disease must be handled to fix your depression. Some drugs, including birth control and some heart medicines, may have depression as a side effect. Your doctor will be prepared to evaluate whether one of your prescriptions is getting you blues and either change your dose or suggest an option.

Medication

Antidepressant drugs are generally prescribed to assist fight severe depression. In the brain, depression is correlated with neurotransmitter abnormalities (chemicals that assist neurons in interacting with other cells). Most antidepressant medications communicate with one or more of the three neurotransmitters that have the biggest impact on mood — serotonin, norepinephrine, and dopamine — to correct an imbalance or weakness that may cause anxiety. There are many different types of antidepressants available, and one type of antidepressant may work better than another for your particular illness. Selective serotonin reuptake drugs (SSRIs) such as Prozac, Zoloft, and Celexa are the most frequently recommended antidepressants. Drugs in this group are efficient for most individuals and generally generate less severe side effects than other kinds of antidepressants: serotonin and norepinephrine reuptake agents (SNRIs), tricyclic and tetracyclic antidepressants, monoamine oxidase agents (MAOIs) and so-called atypical antidepressants such as Wellbutrin. No matter what antidepressant your doctor may prescribe, you can imagine it to wait a few decades before you touch your ancient self again. However, if you do not realize any enhancement after about six weeks or if you have severe side effects, ask your doctor who may recommend you to modify your therapy. Never stop getting your medicine without speaking to your doctor first.

Psychotherapy

Psychotherapy is another pillar of the therapy of depression. Sometimes referred to as' talk therapy,' psychotherapy is characterized by frequent conferences with a psychologist (or a psychologist and a group of other depression sufferers) to know more about depression in specific and your situation in specific. Psychotherapy attempts to describe the factors in a patient's life that may lie at the root of their depression, and relies on teaching a patient on how to avoid the conditions, attitudes, and practices that cause depression. Many people find that just having someone to talk to bits of help to relieve their depression, and some studies suggest that psychotherapy can be just as effective as antidepressant medication in the therapy of mild depression. Psychotherapy is often short-term, lasting only a few weeks after diagnosis, but may last longer if the psychologist or patient thinks it is vital or helpful.

Electroconvulsive Therapy

Electroconvulsive Therapy (ECT) has recovered credibility as a treatment for depression in the latest years. The electrical signals that move through the brain during the ECT trigger an instant seizure, and because the physicians used to hold patients down and zap them without anesthesia, the operation has long been deemed overly invasive, even barbarous. These days, however, physicians are administering the lowest efficient quantity of current while the person is under the influence of general anesthetic and muscle relaxation. The seizure still happens within the brain, causing the required (albeit unknown) modifications in brain chemistry, but without the person needing to convulse or even be conscious of what's going on. ECT is usually suggested in a two-to-four-week course of three drugs per week and is generally reserved for customers who do not get better with antidepressants or whose depression is so severe that they are at danger of harming themselves. The technique is safe and effective for most people but may cause temporary confusion or memory loss.

Stimulation Of The Brain

Stimulation brain initiation is the latest and most experimental type of depression therapy. Multiple kinds of brain stimulation are feasible, but the two most prevalent kinds are vaginal nerve stimulation and deep brain stimulation. Of these, only vagus nerve stimulation has been authorized by the FDA for the treatment of major depression and has stayed contentious. Vagus nervous activity starts with a surgical procedure in which the pulse generator is implanted in the patient's neck, and the wire inside the body links the generator to the vagus nerve in the neck. After surgery, the pulse generator delivers electrical pulses (go figure) to the vagus nerve, which transmits them to the brain, where they can affect the neurotransmitters and gradually improve the mood of the patient. Research has yielded contradictory results, however, and any brain stimulation should only be seen as a last-ditch depression treatment that has demonstrated to be unworkable by any other means.

9 STEPS TO TREAT DEPRESSION NATURALLY

I think that everyone has an opportunity for rehabilitation, even those who have been depressed and worried most of their life.

With my whole core, I wish you excellent health.

1. Identify Any Underlying Conditions

I would try to claim that most individuals with treatment-resistant depression also suffer from undiagnosed circumstances. My list was lengthy: Crohn's disease, tiny intestinal bacterial overgrowth (SIBO), hypothyroidism, high belly acid (hypochlorhydria), adrenal fatigue, Raynaud's syndrome and connective tissue issues, pituitary tumor, aortic valve regurgitation, and certain nutrient deficiencies (iron, vitamin D, and vitamin B-12).

It's best to operate with an integrative or functional doctor. Many of them are mentioned on the Institute of Functional Medicine page, but you need to be cautious because some of them are very costly and will pass useless trials if you are not cautious. At the very least, I would invite your primary care physician or psychologist to perform these four blood exams: complete blood count (CBC); extensive genetic profile (CMP); full thyroid panel, including TSH, free T4, free T3, and thyroid antibodies; and 25-OH vitamin D as well as-12 concentrations. It may also be worth figuring out if you have a mutation in the Methylenetetrahydrofolate reductase (MTHFR) gene (current in 15 to 40 percent of the overall population) because we need the MTHFR enzyme to transform folate to its effective type, methyl folate — and folate deficiencies create it hard for antidepressants to operate. In reality, many trials connect poor folate to depression.

I've discovered more about my different circumstances from individuals at my depression forums, and in books and journals, than I've gained from living in a doctor's office. Project Beyond Blue and Group Beyond Blue are collaborating with nutritionists, integrative physicians, gastrointestinal specialists, and other professionals, and are constantly experimenting with fresh stuff and ready to share their knowledge with you for free. I've discovered from them some of the supplements, protocols, and tools that have helped to mitigate some of my symptoms.

2. Eliminate Triggers of Inflammation

Certain products and medicines cause inflammation in our bodies, including our brains, which contributes to depression. Sugar, gluten, milk, caffeine, and liquor are common suspects. Some individuals, like my sister, may have more drastic responses to milk, while others, like my child, are more influenced by gluten. Me, huh? I can't go near sugar if I don't want the ideas of death to come back. You're not going to understand until you do an elimination diet and get rid of it all for a couple of weeks, and then gradually bring it back in (that is, if you accept it all right). I'm going to warn you, though: you can't cheat for the next few weeks, because your scheme needs to be completely smooth so that you can recognize the issue. A spike in cytokines, proteins that are injected into our bloodstream when our immune system fights off a foreign agent, occurs when individuals are depressed. The method appears the same as when an individual fights any infection. Unfortunately, a bunch of fun, processed products that smell great, like Twinkies and Doritos, can trigger inflammation — but some individuals are more susceptible to others. Here's an easy rule to follow: if the food comes in a nicely marketed package (even with the words "gluten-free," "dairy-free" and ESPECIALLY "sugar free"), and its ingredients contain a bunch of words that you don't know how to pronounce, it won't create you any healthier.

Not to be a complete killjoy, but it's worth checking out what other types of toxins you're immersed in every day. They could also cause inflammation. It wasn't until three months later that I realized that swimming in chlorine a few times a week likely contributed to my intestinal and thyroid problems, both of which are critical to creating a stable mood. So I moved to warm yoga (stage five), and I started to feel better.

3. Go Green

Dark, leafy vegetables like spinach, Swiss chard, and kale boost every device in your body more than any other kind of meals. They are nutrients containing vitamins A, C, E, K and folate; minerals such as iron and calcium; carotenoids; fiber; antioxidants; omega-3s; and phytochemicals. They are also a significant cause of chlorophyll, which, according to Green for Life author Victoria Boutenko, "heals and cleans all our organs, and even kills many of our inner opponents, such as pathogenic bacteria, fungi, cancer cells, and many others." I began to feel a little better when I switched my sandwich at dinner to a salad complete of greens and made a deliberate attempt to consume mood-raising. But I started to cure when I started eating green smoothies. I understand that at this stage I sound like an infomercial, but the only manner my body could readily absorb and handle all the nutrients in the greens was when they were mixed into very tiny bits. Like most individuals who have been on drugs for centuries, my stomach acid was very small, so eating a lot of raw vegetables and greens produced bloating and gas. I wasn't pleased when my spouse spent $500 on a renovated Vitamix, but it proved to be one of the smartest assets we've ever created. Now I attempt to eat two smoothies every day, and I think it has had a significant effect on my health.

4. Heal Your Gut

The complex energetic, nervous system, composed of some 100 million neurons, is embedded in the walls of our intestines, often referred to as our second brain. In reality, the nerve cells in our intestines make up 80 to 90% of our body's serotonin. There is also a complicated set of bacteria residing in our intestines which, according to a large number of studies, affects our mood. It's intriguing things for individuals like me who have always had gastrointestinal issues and never had any points linked before.

5. Do Yoga

Any exercise or motion raises your mood-boosting your brain's dopamine concentrations and supplying endorphins— but some exercises are much more healing than others, particularly for individuals who have been depressed for centuries or have stress-related circumstances like adrenal exhaustion. Unlike other aerobic exercises, such as walking or CrossFit, that increase cortisol concentrations and fundamentally wear out your body, yoga reduces the stress hormone concentrations that are critical to the preservation of homeostasis and the regulation of immune responses, blood sugar, and central nervous system activities. Several trials show how yoga tames the stress response by priming the parasympathetic nervous system and is, therefore, effective therapy for depression and anxiety. I've attempted distinct kinds of yoga, but the one I think most beneficial is Bikram, a series of 26 Hatha yoga roles, and two breathing drills intended to participate and cure all your body's processes. It's not for everyone, as you've been stuck in a space warm to 105 degrees for 90 minutes (sweating helps wipe out the toxins). But when I get there frequently (at least four times a week), I feel a strong, calming effect — and I've heard the same from a few other individuals who are struggling with severe fear and depression.

6. Reduce Stress

Depression is a stress disorder: a disease where stress is poorly controlled by our organs. It's as if many of us with depression and anxiety have a fresh intern seated at the central command of our nervous system, and it keeps categorizing stress reactions wrongly, returning them to the incorrect department in our body. Besides, she stands directly next to the fire alarm and starts blowing every moment there's a sign of distress. But fresh study from the Benson-Henry Institute for Mind-Body Medicine at Massachusetts General Hospital has shown that by generating a soothing reaction, we can instantly change our swelling, metabolism, and insulin-related gene expression — all of which have an effect on our mood. We participate the parasympathetic nervous system with exercise, yoga, profound breathing, massage, and prayer. Even a few lengthy, profound draws when you begin to feel panicked can send a signal to the intern not to sound a fire alarm.

But I've discovered that doing a stress inventory is also critical to working well, an activity where you count on one hand of a sheet of paper everything that makes you feel stressed, and count on the other half everything that enables you to feel easier. Next, you sit down with all that stuff on the left hand of the document (what's stressing) and have a violently candid conversation with yourself about why you're doing it (people-pleasing hang-ups? ego? mistaken targets?), accompanied by a meeting where you discover innovative alternatives to get as many out of it as you can. I had a stress inventory with myself a few months ago, when I finally admitted that my health wasn't worth trying to become a blogging celebrity and best-selling author like Gretchen Rubin, as I've always wanted to be, or running a terrific non-profit like BringChange2Mind. It was an epiphany moment when I realized that I don't have to be someone else to be OK. By operating at my snail velocity, I've had enough time to do more on the right side of the paper to make me feel good.

7. Take the Right Supplements

It may be overwhelming to attempt to figure out which supplements might be helpful and how to distinguish between quality products consumer Lab lists fifth party-tested substitutes which need to be guaranteed. I also conducted some studies and discovered that these companies were reputable: Prothera, Klaire Labs, Pure Encapsulations, Douglas Laboratories, Nature Made, Orthomolecular Products, Metagenics, Vital Nutrients, Truehope, OmegaBrite and Carlson Laboratories.

In a friend article, she mentioned some Patient-Approved Natural Supplements for Depression; she mention a variety of vitamins and minerals that are beneficial to your mood. But here are the critical things that I'd begin with: omega-3 medicines, probiotics, vitamin D, vitamin-12, and multivitamins. Because I have poor stomach acid (as do many individuals who have been on drugs for years), I get more outcomes when I bring a cloud of dust or a liquid. I'm getting my vitamin D and B-12 from Pure Prescriptions as a liquid. Blogger Lisa Richards has created an excellent roster of the best company probiotics, her favorite being Healthy Origins 30 Billion or Prescript-Assist. I take Ther-Biotic Complete Powder because it contains all the different kinds of bacteria I need for my unique intestinal disease (Crohn plus significant intestinal bacteria).

 A few months earlier, I began getting a multivitamin called EmpowerPlus Powder from TrueHope after reading through all the study papers using this particular micronutrient to assist manage various mood disorders and observing Julia Rucklidge's inspirational TEDx talk about nutrition and micronutrients. Finally, I get my omega-3 complement from OmegaBrite because its capsules contain

70% EPA (eicosapentaenoic acid) at a proportion of 7:1 EPA to DHA (docosahexaenoic acid). A new study has verified the beneficial impacts of EPA on mood, even more so than DHA, since it offers a natural equilibrium to omega-6 arachidonic acid. Nordic Naturals is a credible brand as well. If you do have a mutation of the MTHFR gene, it is a good idea to complement the bioavailable type of folate with l-methyl folate.

8. Protect Your Sleep

From all my research on mood disorders over the last ten years and conversations with people who can't get well, I'd claim chronic stress and interrupted sleep patterns are the two greatest variables that stop an individual from getting out of the depths of depression. Unfortunately, when there is depression, there are generally problems with sleep. Volumes of research have recorded the disastrous impacts of exercise on mental health, such as that of the American Academy of Sleep Medicine, which discovered that the heritability of depressive diseases in twins with very brief sleep was almost twice the heritability of twins sleeping seven to nine hours a night.

Because I am such a delicate animal, I had to shift bed up on my priority list from No. 7 to No. 1. With everything I've got, I safeguard it. This means that I won't wake up at 5 a.m. To get the job out. I bed, I exercise afterward, and I'm a lot less effective during the day (phase six). But working 8 hours a weekend allows me more resilient to mood swings. I had to adopt strict sleep hygiene rules to ensure that I didn't end up with the kind of miserable insomnia that I had two years ago: I shut down the computer at 7 p.m., leave my phone downstairs (not next to my touch) and don't inspect messages after 8 p.m., and try to remain in bed by 10 p.m. It's all evening. I also started using lavender oil, getting melatonin, and a combination of magnesium and calcium at dusk, which seems to calm me down.

9. Find a Purpose

Nietzsche said, "He who has a reason to live can bear almost any way." Last summer, when I began to think that I would never be without weakening death's thoughts, I clung to that logic, and the inspiring words of the Holocaust survivor and the famous psychiatrist Viktor Frankl, MD, Ph.D. If a person has found a purpose in life, he explains in his classic Man's Search for Meaning, "even the helpers." So I began my two forums and a non-profit organization devoted to treatment-resistant depression. They haven't healed me of my symptoms, but I can honestly claim that to commit to a goal last summer is what gave me hope in an era of despair. For the first moment, I could see myself having a meaningful life in spite of the constant ruminations that clogged my brain. When I started helping someone else out of the cliff, I often forgot about my fascination with jumping. I believe Nietzsche and Frankl are correct about that. Meaning and intent can function as a kind of anesthesia of pain; concentrating on your tiny position in making the globe a stronger place to position your suffering in a broader view that contributes to peace.

Chapter 14

BONUS: HOW TO HELP TEENS WITH ANXIETY AND DEPRESSION

Just as adults often suffer from anxiety, kids and adolescents may also suffer from anxiety. Sometimes this anxiety is caused by stressful or traumatic occurrences, but often it is not possible to identify a particular stressor.

While there are many anxiety disorders, generalized anxiety disorder, and social anxiety disorder are more prevalent in kids and adolescents. These kids are anxious and have problems in social circumstances. Anxiety often manifests itself as Separation Anxiety Disorder and Specific Phobia in very young kids. These symptoms often include an excellent deal of hesitation to separate from carers and multiple, seemingly unjustified, concerns.

Teens respond differently to diseases than adolescents with comparable anxiety issues, which can render diagnosis very hard. It may also be difficult to distinguish between a "stage" or reasonable problem and real disease. In either situation, it can have a significant impact on the child's feeling of well-being and accomplishment in college.

Because adolescence is a moment of mood swings and furious outbursts accompanied by tearful withdrawals, it is tough to say if your teenager is just a typical teenager or if their conduct is reflective of a more significant issue. Anxiety disorders in kids and adolescents are often ignored. This can be dangerous supervision as overly distressed adolescents transform into too anxious adolescents, or even more severely, a specter of depression and suicide.

While having distinct physical and emotional adjustments in the pre-adolescence and adolescence stages, both men and women experience a certain amount of stress and anxiety. In other words, growing up can be a hard feeling for both sexes. These physical changes trigger specific mental make-up, a modified approach towards individuals and the conditions around them. These teenage kids are not sufficiently ready to deal with stress during these temporary stages.

Causes, Connections, And What Parents Can Do To Help

Teen depression is on the increase, and the best approach of the parent to assist the kid is to foster the growth of critical skills.

One of the most significant elements of healing and recovery, be it from accident, anxiety or broken heart, is the conviction that change is feasible. Researchers call this "favorable expectation" and, when we look at the achievement of treatment, it is essential.

To do the hard work of altering or healing, we must think that change is genuinely an alternative. Recently, I've been bumping into more and more data about depression and anxiety disorders that says the precise contrary of that.

In an attempt to encourage consciousness of mental health and to encourage kids, adolescents and adults to find assistance with mental health problems, posts that depression and anxiety disorders are brain diseases that "just occur" and, more worryingly, "how you're wired" or "are like diabetes and heart illness" have come up again and again. Drug ads are significant perpetrators, but they are not the only ones. (Note: I am not speaking about bipolar disorder or schizophrenia... they are regarded and handled differently.)

Seeing Teen Depression For What It Is

I know the intention: we want to avoid children and adolescents from feeling guilty or embarrassed when they are fighting.

We want them to know that mental health problems like this are prevalent and treatable. We don't want them to feel lonely. But they also understand critically that their bodies are malleable and changeable.

The way we believe, evolve, connect to others, and address difficulties are critical to excellent mental health and are part of our human experience that can be taught, unlearned and adjusted.

What you think in yourself and how you perceive the globe are essential considerations in both the growth and rehabilitation from fear, depression, stress, messy interactions and many other problems.

Teens are hearing — so they inform me when I question them — that depression and fear are constant, depending on complicated wiring and genes. While there may be some genetic input to anxiety and depression in teenagers, there is no recognized anxiety gene or depression gene, or any robust scientific evidence that thoroughly explains what creates depression.

We understand that the malleability of our bodies, our chemistry, and even the genetic expression of our DNA is far broader and more critical than the scientists thought 10 or 15 years earlier, and we understand about danger variables, such as trauma, confinement, and cultural disconnection, to name a few.

Depression Is Not Who You Are

Rather than encouraging the right adjustments in thinking, acting, decision-making, and connectivity, we are hindering the favorable expectations and motivation that are crucial to addressing these issues. And we are inhibiting a significant debate of danger variables, avoidance, and rehabilitation.

When we offer the teenagers a signal that "this is who they are," that their brains are imbalanced, and that depression is a "just show up" disease, our efforts to assist are probably doing the precise contrary.

Depression and anxiety in adolescents are very genuine and harmful when left alone, but a therapy that relies on constructing funds and abilities is beneficial.

Connecting Teen Depression and Anxiety

As an anxiety specialist, I often speak to teenagers who are also depressed. Why? Why?

Because a child's untreated anxiety disorder is one of the main predictors of adolescent or young adult depression, most teenagers and relatives are unaware of it. And because anxiety is young people's primary mental health issue, it's not surprising that teen depression levels are rising.

Adolescence is often a moment when long-term problems with anxiety and anxiety become more intense and isolating. The difficulties of social existence and enhanced scholarly pressure are driving children towards new lives and obligations, along with the shadows of hesitation and insecurity.

Specific learning difficulties may arise as learners take on more complex assignments or have to talk up in school. Sports are becoming more challenging, and hormones can wreak havoc with their appearance. Whether social, mental, or physical, anything can serve as a cause of concern.

Teens are caught between wanting to accomplish and fearing failure, wanting to be part of, and fearing refusal.

When teenagers think that they will not weigh up or expect refusal, they leave.

To make things worse, adolescents are more inclined to dismiss adult feedback as they strive to be autonomous and to discover their responses. At a moment when they are confronted with enormous adjustments–graduating from high college, hoping to hear from schools, going away from home or choosing a professional path–your recommendation and willingness to assist are being encountered with opposition.

No degree of reassurance or encouragement seems to be enough because you can't offer your child what she's looking for: an assurance that everything is going to work out ultimately.

The Desire For Certainty

And this wish for assurance enables anxiety to catch your adolescent and hang on firmly. Add to that a competing willingness to be component of a complex and unsure social world, and it is no surprise that the removal, despair, and sorrow of depression can take hold.

This implies that assisting kids and adolescents in recognizing and normalizing the difficulties of interactions, issue solving, frustration and uncertainty is crucial to avoidance and rehabilitation. These are the abilities that could and should be learned.

Your worried adolescent is looking for a certainty that everything is going to work out ultimately. Since you can not regulate it, the objective of the community is to accept it with ease.

Shifting Thought Patterns

When we speak about permanence and disease, we lose a chance. We need to assist our kids in recognizing and responding to habits of thinking that can be most helpful and most hurtful.

For instance, most adolescents know that lives can be volatile. But during this moment of flux, they sometimes lose their capacity to accept such significant uncertainties.

Many anxious teens become stuck by the following rigid patterns when creating plans and thinking about the future:

Perfectionism: "All must—and can be done perfectly."

Catastrophic thinking: "If one thing goes right, it's all going to fall apart, and I'm not going to be happy in life."

The One Path Myth: "There's one PATH to a good existence. I have to discover it or remain on it, no matter how!"

How To Help A Teen With Depression

These forms of thinking generate anxiety and stress in teenagers, so what can you do as a parent to assist? You can begin by paying attention to how you and your family are dealing with failures and errors.

Research informs us persuasively that your interaction with fear and uncertainty— and how you design this on your child— has a significant impact on how she views the universe.

When is there something beautiful enough? How are you going to proceed on to your next assignment? What's your household saying about the screw-ups?

Now maybe the moment to recognize and alter your reaction to errors, to sprinkle family conversations with sentences that normalize screw-ups, battles, and imperfections.

Teens also need to hear that they're not expected to know everything and that they can't see the future.

The objective is NOT to create all the right choices. The aim is to have the problem-solving abilities required to adapt from the inevitable poor ones.

Flexibility is the key, and this implies learning when to work harder and when to be happy with a less than perfect consequence. As you see your child becoming nervous, look for chances to let her understand that this is a moment of uncertainty, but you have trust in her capacity to fix problems along with the manner.

Giving guidance on how you're going to manage stuff may not be as useful as instilling a feeling of independence in your teen— and this may imply cutting off the lessons and allowing her to understand that you're there to help her as she takes her decisions.

Worry Is Normal

In the end, teenagers need to know that they should be nervous! It is unrealistic to expect to be calm and comfortable during such a moment of transition.

In reality, going towards anxiety and teaching how to handle it is the ability that I am most heavily committed to.

If a child thinks that keeping calm is the objective, she will prevent taking hazards, remain where she is most relaxed, and never create up her feeling of trust.

Let her feel her emotions, but then encourage her to take action and bravely move into uncertainty. Although your first instinct may be to jump in and create it all right, understand that you are equipping your child with precious abilities when you model and promote a more flexible — and independent— adulthood route.

Remember how teenagers were told kids were better at math and science? And then did they live up to those restricted hopes? We're not doing that anymore.

Unfortunately, however, we have substituted these old brain myths with some fresh ones. With the rate of depression and anxiety among college learners at an all-time high, we need to begin paying attention to the strength and (in) accuracy of our language about transition, intelligence, and the future of our children's mental health.

Learning how to assist a teenager with anxiety and depression implies learning the abilities required to solve problems to react to the hard choices and the poor decisions they all make.

Help teenagers to step away from their strict expectations and continuous thinking, and instead help them through this moment of the fight, pain, discovery, and development with the language of transition, change, and motion.

Most importantly, remain attached to your teenagers, even when you know how awkward you are.

Small movements go a lengthy way: give a tip, ask a query or two that conveys real concern, and be that constant stream of texts that let them understand that you're there when they need to travel, drop, regroup, and discover their way.

What Parents Can Do To Help

Fear of what other individuals might say, or be laughed at, or not taken seriously, can often prevent young individuals from getting the first step in acknowledging that they need assistance. That's why it's so essential that families and loved ones understand the methods in which kids can struggle and give approaches to assist them deal with and handle their stress at home.

Here, David Brudö from the Personal Development and Mental Wellness App Remente describes how fathers can best sustain their kid through a hard time.

Knowing The Signs

When it goes to adolescents, it can be hard to understand the distinction between a poor mood associated with hormonal modifications and a miserable feeling that is a sign of a significant mental health disorder, such as anxiety or depression. The easiest way to understand if a person is depressed is to see if you notice a noticeable distinction in their behavior–if they no longer do the stuff they appreciate, if their educational achievement suffers, or if their poor mood lasts longer than a few weeks, it could be an indication of a mental health problem.

Learn To Listen To Them

If your adolescent begins speaking to you about how they feel, create an attempt to hear to them, without being too critical of them or overbearing in your concern. While you may contact the desire to guide or share information, they want to learn that they can talk to you and that you recognize their emotions, without judging them. Knowing that you're there for them, promoting them, can do a lot to assist a depressed or distressed adolescent.

Learn To Discuss

When a teenager feels nervous or depressed, they may not recognize emotions about what they are, thinking that something is wrong with them, that they are' fragile' or' crazy.' You must teach yourself first, and then you teach them on these circumstances. For instance, anxiety can often come along with physical signs such as a feeling sick, a rushing pulse, and a sensation of clammy. Once the adolescent knows that what they're going through is ordinary, they're more inclined to open up and talk to you, without fear of disappointing you.

Stay Present

When it goes to adolescents, it's no wonder to adolescents that a lot of their lives are spent on their smartphone, tablet or computer. Social media is a two-edged sword, in the sense that it helps us remain attached to buddies, but in another it can have weak self-esteem and a position of useless violence on the part of colleagues. As you help your child through anxiety or depression, you must stay active. Dedicate time to both of you sitting down and speaking or doing something enjoyable, with no social media distractions or messages from either of you. The adolescent is going to get a break from their display and your undivided attention, which they need to open up to you.

Don't Think About Physical Health

Many times, mental health problems can be exacerbated by bad physical health, particularly in adolescents who may have uneven sleep habits, a lot of screen time, and junk food. As an adult, you can create sure they're receiving enough practice by proposing operations that you can do together, or that they're going to sleep on time. Similarly, adolescents who have anxiety may also lose interest in eating owing to the absence of appetite, which is why you must maintain track of their food and nutrition.

Seek Assistance

Often, it can be enough to ask your kid what they believe might help them feel better and alter. However, they may not be willing to talk to you about their issues, or they may not understand what they can do to assist. It may be difficult for a family to know that they might not be willing to help, so know when to seek skilled assistance. If you are profoundly worried, you should meet your GP–your kid may have a one-on-one session with them, or you can speak about your issues and ask for advice.

Look After Yourself

Parenting can be challenging and stressful at moments, and you must look after your mental health because it can only have a beneficial effect on your family. Think about how you display your feelings of rage and anxiety in front of your children because they're probably to take a bunch of behavioral signals from you.

Try Free Apps

Free-to-use applications like Remente to give teenagers a way to access mental health on the go. The app mixes psychology with brain and spiritual instruction to assist consumers achieve their full capacity, finish their objectives, and pursue a healthier lifestyle. Teens can monitor their mood through the app as well as conduct stress management and goal setting classes.

CONCLUSION

In the past, you questioned yourself, "You can cure depression." More specifically, you've wondered "may depression be healed naturally." I hope this manual will give you the response you've been looking for... but what comes next is up to you.

You can hit your depression if you want to. But you've got to create a clear choice.

No more, "I would like to" or "It would be good."

Shouldn't beat illnesses, only' Musts' can do that.

You've got the authority to win this. You were not born depressed, and if you're willing to fight your way out of your teeth and claws, you don't have to be depressed.

You must fight this as if it were a battle for your existence, because, quite honestly, it is. Life's too brief to withstand depression. It's too valuable to spend another second feeling sorry for yourself and living in a state of pain.

Switch the "should" to the "must."

If you're suffering from depression, there's only one task and one task... Win. Reclaim your joy, your happiness, your life. You don't have to endure, and if you're prepared to take action on what I've experienced with you, you're not.

You can defeat this one. You're going to defeat this.

Now, get after it.

Do Not Go Yet; One Last Thing To Do

If you enjoyed this book or found it useful I'd be very grateful if you'd post a short review on Amazon. Your support really does make a difference and I read all the reviews personally so I can get your feedback and make this book even better.

Thanks again for your support!